LAURA ASHLEY
COLOR

LAURA ASHLEY

COLOR

Using Color to Decorate Your Home

SUSAN BERRY

Special Photography by David Brittain

CLARKSON POTTER/PUBLISHERS

NEW YORK

Published by Clarkson N. Potter, Inc./Publishers, East 50th Street, New York, New York, 10022.
Member of the Crown Publishing Group.

Random House, Inc. New York, Toronto, London, Sydney, Auckland
www.randomhouse.com

Clarkson N. Potter, Potter, and colophon are tradmarks of Clarkson N. Potter, Inc.

First published in the United Kingdom in 1995 by Ebury Press
Random House, 20 Vauxhall Bridge Road, London SW1V 2SA

First pubished in hardcover in the United States in 1995 by Harmony Books, a division of Crown Publishers, Inc., 201 East 50th Street, New York, New York, 10022. Member of the Crown Publishing Group.

First paperback edition printed in 1998.

Printed in Portugal

Library of Congress Cataloging-in-Publication Data
Berry, Susan
Laura Ashley Color: Using Color to Decorate Your Home / Susan Berry ; special photography by David Brittain.

Color in interior decoration I. Laura Ashley (Firm)
NK2115.5.c6B47   1998
-dc21

Project Editor: Jane Struthers
Pages 74-5, 96-7, 104-5, 156-7, 166-7 and 196-7 by Allison Wormleighton
Designed by Christine Wood
Special photography by David Brittain
Styling by Jacky Boase
Picture research by Emily Hedges

ISBN 0-609-80375-1

10 9 8 7 6 5 4 3 2 1

First Paperback Edition

Contents

Introduction

In some respects, the use of color has come full circle since Laura Ashley's initial success in home furnishings in the late 1970s. The image that most people conjure up when they think of traditional Laura Ashley decoration is of a romantic country bedroom decorated in small floral prints. These were dress prints used in the same way that the French use *toile de Jouy*–using a blue print on a white ground for the walls, and a white print on a blue ground for the curtains–and they gave Laura Ashley its distinctive country look. This was essentially monochrome decorating, which was very popular in the 1970s, and has since seen a return to fashion in the 1990s.

Just as the Arts and Crafts movement of the nineteenth century had looked to natural colors rather than synthetic ones, Laura Ashley's original color palette reflected the naturalness of the country, and the use of natural dyes. The range featured browns such as oak and saddle, earth colors, terra-cotta and cream, navy and burgundy, muted mid-tone colors such as smoke and plum, and, for a more masculine look, dark green on white. These colors worked well with the warm tones of stripped pine, terra-cotta tiles, the simplicity of brass beds on bare floorboards, rag rugs and a nostalgia for an idealized life in the country before the advent of the modern age.

These colors were designed to work on their own in decorating, although there were some natural color groupings, such as the browns with terra-cotta, and smoke with plum. There were no rules, particularly as to which colors suited which rooms, so navy was as acceptable in a bedroom as plum and rose. Other colors were introduced, and a bright color palette reflected contemporary decorating trends. Poppy red, apple green, bright yellow mustard, and china blue were all easy and bright to use in kitchens and bathrooms, and also in children's bedrooms.

In the early 1980s, soft pastel colors–including pale pink, rose, sapphire blue, and apricot–were introduced and remained extremely popular throughout the decade. The prints themselves were developed to include more colors, and the color palette became much more sophisticated. Combinations of colors were important in creating different looks–a particularly crucial point was varying the shade of green used in the foliage of floral prints so that it would work with the main color. Rose and sapphire were linked with moss green, smoke and plum with a dirty sage, and a pale aquamarine was combined with a rich apricot.

At first, the decorating story was simple, but by the second half of the 1980s, the chintz

This Louis XVI bedroom in a French chateau was decorated by Laura Ashley in 1984 to introduce a new blue, called kingfisher, to the collection. The fabric is called Antoinette and the design was based on a French eighteenth-century silk print.

room had introduced riots of color as fabrics reflected the flower borders in country house gardens. The romantic cottage had turned into the romantic country house. The pastels developed into many more varieties of shades and tones. Navy, burgundy, and dark green replaced brown at the darker end of the color spectrum, but were now used with a sand background, rather than white, for a more sophisticated, traditional look redolent of country house libraries.

At the end of the 1980s, cowslip yellow became very fashionable. After the popularity of pastel colors earlier in the decade, there was a need for something brighter, but not primary, and cowslip yellow was perfect. Two particularly popular designs were Laura Ashley's Lyme Regis wallpaper in cowslip, and the Alba Roses chintz, which is a striking floral bouquet spaced on a white ground, and on a larger scale than many of the earlier designs. Many other designs in cowslip followed, the most notable of which was Sweet Pea, which combined various tones of cowslip and sapphire blue in a stunning, sunny, floral print that was particularly popular.

Many colors have been introduced for specific purposes—a warmer red, a clearer blue, heath green which is more yellow than the blue-green jade, and different shades of white for varying grounds to fabrics and wallpapers. Colors have also been introduced for individual collections, such as jade, crimson, and ivory for the Chinoiserie Collection, and midnight blue and gold for a theme based on Venetian and Renaissance designs.

More recently, color versus non-color has become a big design issue. Taupe, which was introduced as a background color in some multi-colored floral prints in the 1980s, took over as the basis for a whole range of neutral colors that have become the vogue in the early 1990s. Alongside this has been the faded florals look, where all the tones of differing colors have been equalized to give the effect of having been aged by the sun. This makes them look instantly at home in a decorating scheme. In contrast, the bright, rich colors of hot climates, from India to the South of France, are evident—chambray blue and plaster pink, ochers and russets, deep pinks and rich blues.

In general, in relation to decorating, people have become much more adventurous and knowledgeable since Laura Ashley was first in business, and color has emerged as the most important element in home design for the 1990s. This book will help you to understand color better, appreciate the subtleties of particular hues, and enhance your decorating skills in a variety of different ways.

ABOVE *This new print in cowslip, called Paeony, was launched in 1992. Cowslip is still a popular decorating color.*

BELOW *This kitchen shows the Kitchen Garden print in plaster pink, a marvelous 1990s color.*

CHAPTER 1

living with color

It is surprising how many people who are fairly confident and assured about their taste, lose all that confidence when trying to mix and match colors. Instead of following their instincts, and deciding what appeals to them and what they enjoy looking at, they become indecisive and ill-at-ease. In fact, there are no fixed rules when it comes to color and it pays to forget all those old adages you learned at your grandmother's knee–that blue and green should never be seen, and that red and orange clash. So much depends not only on color, but on shape, texture, the amount of color used, and the amount and type of light in the room too.

When it comes to interior decorating, the sheer scale on which the color is seen can be extremely confusing. What looks good in a paint sample not much bigger than the bristles on a paintbrush might be too dominating or too insipid when spread over an enormous expanse of wall. Equally, colors that do not go together when seen in small amounts, held close together, can blend and harmonize surprisingly well when they are some distance from each other in a large room. Using a patterned fabric that contains the two colors you wish to use can be a good way to unify the decorating scheme if you are unsure of the effect they will create on their own.

If you are used to color-matching clothes, where the amounts of color and fabric involved are relatively small, it may come as a great surprise that you have a lot more scope as an interior decorator. It is not as important to match the exact tone or shade of a color in a room as it is in an outfit, although you must be aware of the long-distance effect. People do not walk into a room and examine a pillow from a distance of about 2 feet (60 cm), as you may do when choosing one in a department store. They notice, or fail to notice, the effect from about 10 feet (3 meters), and the object will be surrounded by other colors, surfaces, and textures, all of which may harmonize with or detract from the object in question.

This is why coordinated ranges, such as those produced by Laura Ashley, can be so helpful. They provide the color scheme upon which the room can be based. You might wish to use a particular curtain fabric, choosing the paint and wallpaper in complementary designs, and then picking out one or two of the main colors in the rest of the room. However, it is important to use a coordinated range carefully, leaving scope for adding your own personality and keeping the very element of decorating that makes it such fun–the individuality. In order to be able to do this successfully, you need to identify the key colors in the range, and then find either toning or harmonizing colors or one that provides a clear contrast. However, it is important that you make sure you do not introduce more than one color to the scheme, or it may start to look fragmented.

It is the illusory nature of color that causes so many problems to the would-be colorist or decorator, since colors are not static—our perception of them alters so that the effect differs according to the circumstances in which we see them. Colors also affect each other, so the way you combine colors can alter the way you perceive them. For example, cowslip yellow on its own will look like a simple, fresh yellow. If you put a similar area of black next to it, it will look harder, and if you put an area of red next to it, it will look much warmer.

This, as you can see, makes an enormous difference to your decorating schemes. Another important consideration is light. Light changes when it strikes different surfaces. When light strikes a black surface, most of it is absorbed. When light strikes a white surface, most of it is reflected. An opaque, colored surface absorbs some frequencies of the spectrum and reflects others.

Color is light perceived by the retina of the human eye, and light is a series of wavelengths. In very dim conditions, what you see has no color at all. At higher light levels, these wavelengths are bent or refracted by differing amounts within our eyes to produce what we know as the color spectrum. The most visible manifestation of the color spectrum is, of course, the rainbow in which the order of the colors is always the same—red, orange, yellow, green, blue, and violet. In fact, violet and red are at opposite ends of the spectrum and the colors in between are simply deviations.

The principles of color

This monochromatic color scheme in classic navy and gold uses bold pattern in a restrained and elegant way to create a sophisticated, yet strong, color scheme. The beautifully dressed windows, with swagged valance in a navy and sand check fabric, create the focal point. The chairs are upholstered in plain cream and classic broad stripes of navy and white. Touches of bright gold, in the picture frames and tie-backs, add vitality to the decorative scheme.

The different types and colors of light have specific terms:

- Hue is the term used to differentiate pure colors.
- Brightness indicates the range from light to dark.
- Intensity indicates the range from a pure hue to one in which light or dark (white or black) is mixed with it.
- Tints describe the range from a pure hue to white.
- Shades indicate the range from a pure hue to black.
- Tones are the range from a pure hue to gray.
- Saturation is the term used to describe the degree of brilliance or brightness of a hue.

The psychology of color

As well as physically perceiving color, you also respond psychologically to color, mostly in the same way. In other words, colors create changes of mood, which are more or less universal, in the beholder. Generally speaking, yellow lifts the spirits and induces a feeling of cheerfulness; black depresses the spirits, as can brown and purple. Red creates a strong reaction–some people find it energizing, others find it overpowering–but either way it is not a restful color, which green is. Green soothes. Blue induces moods of reflectivity and tranquility. White appears pure, but may not be particularly restful. The shades in between these colors will vary in their effect and impact according to how much of the other colors they contain.

In certain situations, the psychology of color has been employed quite deliberately by professional designers, for example both in interior decorating and in packaging. Red is the color of danger and of urgency, which is why the sign for the Red Cross is red on a white ground. Equally, red is the color of fire and passion, which is why so many red flowers are sent around Valentine's Day.

Colors also have symbolic connotations as well as psychological significance, although the symbolism varies according to the country in question. In the West, white is the color of purity and is therefore a traditional choice for weddings. In Latin America, purple is the color of death. In Moslem countries, green is a holy color.

Certain colors are also perceived to be masculine or feminine. Generally, darker colors and stronger hues–such as dark greens, reds, and navys–are masculine, while pastels and paler hues–such as apple greens, pinks, and powder blues–are seen as feminine. However, combining the two with a novel contrasting color–such as tobacco brown with pink, or fuchsia pink with dark green–or using a masculine, geometric pattern with the pinks and a floral pattern with the dark greens, can subtly alter the usual psychological connotations.

The dramatic colors of fall are shown here, with the scarlet leaves of the Japanese maple forming a vivid still life. Nature often provides inspiration for stunning color schemes.

Color balance

Generally, the most successful schemes have a limited palette of two or three principal colors, perhaps with touches here and there of other colors. If you want to vary the atmosphere, a tonal decorating scheme can be very effective—you can use several tones of one color (adding white or black to the color, but not changing the basic hue—in other words not adding a particular color). This is especially successful with a very limited palette—perhaps one color—as it breaks up the monotony and adds texture, depth, and vibrancy to the whole scheme. It has been used by many successful interior designers and is very effective for highlighting architectural detailing.

It is important, when using more than one color, to think carefully about color balance. How much of any one color do you want to use, and to what extent will it dominate the other colors used? As a rule of thumb, the brighter the color, the smaller the amount of it that you should use, as it will tend to overwhelm any duller colors that accompany it. If, for example, your scheme is mainly the color that in the eighteenth century was called drab (this is a dirty khaki, and goes with a surprising number of other hues) matched with, for example, very small amounts of a bright cobalt blue, you will have a distinguished-looking scheme. If, on the other hand, you opted for large quantities of bright cobalt blue with touches of drab, the result would quite different. That is because it is the proportions that count when color-mixing, not only the colors used. Quantities are therefore extremely important in this delicate matter of color combining, and it is not an easy point to grasp until you see a successful scheme translated into its negative image. It then becomes clear why one works and the other does not.

Mixing colors

Companies like Laura Ashley introduce new colorways and new designs in their collections each year. Their designers have professional expertise in mixing color and pattern, and you can use this to your advantage by choosing their pre-mixed colors and patterns. You can, if you wish, redecorate your home each time you see a new textile design that you like but, if you prefer, you can gradually mix different colors, patterns, and fabrics yourself to create a more personalized look that you can add to as it suits you. The aim of this chapter is to help you to do just that, by telling you the principles that interior decorators use when mixing color, so that you have some basis on which to plan and design a scheme yourself.

Combining several colors and patterns in a decorative scheme is certainly not new—the Victorians took it to a high art in their color schemes known as polychromy—but it requires more discipline and a better eye than simply limiting the color scheme to one, or perhaps two, colors. For the less sure, a limited color scheme is definitely a valid starting point for a simplified design.

Multicolored effects, however, look most effective when based on an inherent plan. First, you need to decide which colors you will combine—but how do you make this initial, elementary choice? Inspiration for colors, and color schemes, can be found in the most unexpected places. The secret is to take note of the objects that surround you—both in your own home and in the landscape—and to see which colors inspire you, or fire your imagination. There are myriad color hues to choose from, and the differences between them can be very subtle indeed. Nature usually provides us with the best source of inspiration—from flowers and fruit to fields and landscapes—but there are man-made sources too, many of which are associated with design and decoration, from fine art and architecture, the decorative arts, furniture, ceramics, packaging, and trends in the fashion world through to the printed textiles we use in interior decoration.

Keeping a notebook in which to write down items or colors of particular interest will help, and you may find that you develop a particular taste or inclination toward a certain range of colors, or particular light or dark tones, which help to define your own taste. The color collages (see pages 27–37) illustrate the spectrum of colors at your disposal, and have been made of up of a variety of items, both textiles and paints, and natural sources of color and texture, to illustrate how texture and pattern can affect color.

In days gone by, you were usually advised not to mix patterns (and, as a consequence, colors), because of the clashes you were likely to create. Pattern-mixing has become far more fashionable now, and the variety of patterns available has made it easier, but it still requires careful planning to make it work. However, there are certain basic principles

Strong primary colors–blue, red, and yellow–require a bold treatment. Here, the contrast between fully saturated (i.e. colors at their brightest) blues, reds, and yellows helps to ensure that the colors work well together, with no single color dominating. The use of purple, for the pillows, helps to bridge the gap between the red and blue and bring them into harmony (purple is made from red and blue), while the large expanses of plain color draw your attention to the textures in the room–glossy silks, sheeny walls, translucent curtains and rough sisal on the floor.

you can follow that will help to ensure success, and they are described here.

The best method is to choose a series of colors that are balanced in some way–a similar intensity of hue, for example–and that ideally leave white out of the equation unless you are mixing neutral colors together. Used with stronger or brighter colors, white tends to be divisive and may create the jarring, restless effect that you need to avoid when playing with several color combinations. Nevertheless, white and shades of off-white, especially when used for ceilings, can lighten a room and make the colors appear more vivid. The use, or exclusion, of white in a decorative scheme will depend on the effect you wish to create and, probably, the amount of natural light in the room.

Good choices for a mixed color palette include claret, forest green, classic navy, and gold; speedwell blue, taupe, and cream; and pale plaster pink, olive green, chambray blue, and ocher. Mixing more than four colors is probably pushing your luck a little too far. Two other considerations are the quantities of colors being used and the proportions of the room. You should try to avoid using equal amounts of each color; instead, focus attention on two colors as the major theme, and use the other color in the supporting role as an accent color.

As with painting, the aim is to ensure that any color you use is not employed in isolation but is picked up as a leitmotif of the whole scheme. If you have used ocher for

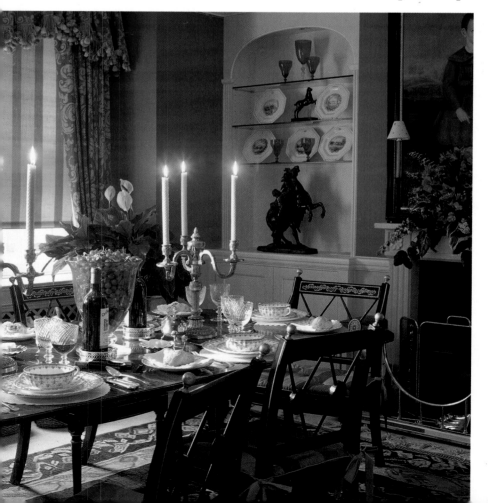

the walls, make sure that it reappears again in a background pattern on, say, the cushions. A dusty pink used for the frieze and ceiling could be repeated in a patterned fabric that picks out ocher, pink, and one of the other colors–perhaps blue. Simple stripes of blue and pink could be used for one chair; the same fabric in an ocher and green colorway could be used for another chair, that has a similar shape.

Regency stripes have long been a popular choice for dining rooms. Here they are given a new twist in terra-cotta and cream rather than in the more familiar combination of vermilion and white, and are used for the blinds rather than the walls. The effect is more subtle and restrained, while still having a strong classical feeling. The colors are a wonderful foil for the oil painting over the fireplace.

Neutral color schemes can work very well with antique furniture and classic surroundings, as this simple and restrained dining room proves. Wallpaper is often eschewed in neutrals schemes, but here it works brilliantly in a monochromatic design. The antiqued cream fireplace is the perfect complement to the fine paintings and antique furniture.

Ensuring that there is a connection of form and/or color is one of the secrets of avoiding fragmentation in such a scheme. In other words, try to repeat the shapes of, say, the soft furnishings when using mixed colors to keep some kind of continuity in the room. Alternatively, if you are using a fairly simple color palette, you could introduce different outlines and forms of furnishing to add visual interest. Another secret it is important to remember is the use of similar types of wood or fabrics. It is best not to use several kinds of wood as well as a range of fabric types and weights. For the latter, keep to simple cottons, or perhaps luxurious silks and velvets. Mixing colors and fabric types is likely to lead to a disturbing clash of ideas. Keep the contrasts of materials for the more uniform schemes–changing the texture in a neutrals scheme, for example, is the key to bringing this type of scheme to life.

Painted surfaces give you the chance to experiment with combinations of different tones and colors: you can use stencils, rubber stamps, or wooden blocks to create a wide range of patterns with subtle or distinct variations within the same hue, and without using white as a contrast. Again, picking out one color from a multicolored stencil (composed perhaps of taupe, olive, blue, and sand) for the paintwork (in olive) would allow you to use more than one color, but in a discreet and unobtrusive way. You could use these particular colors in various soft pattern combinations of stripes, checks, and florals, provided you kept the tonal values much the same. The scheme would not work if you used several shades of the same color. When using three or more colors, therefore, it becomes increasingly important to keep the tonal values the same. When using one color, you can increase the interest by using three or more tones.

Try mixing lots of pale sorbet colors together, such as apple green, sapphire blue, pale yellow, and powder pink. Then add plenty of white to keep the scheme light before adding an accent color of deep pink or turquoise. Alternatively, you could use lots of very light tones, such as pale cream, pale yellow, and white, for the walls and furniture, and then add a dark accent color such as navy blue or forest green. You could try the decorative scheme in reverse, with a dark blue room and burgundy and green upholstery, and add splashes of gold and cream highlights. You could mix solid blocks of bright colors for a jazzy effect, or mix tones of dark colors. The options are endless. Some examples of the different effects that are created by using lighter and darker tones in a decorative scheme are shown on pages 44–49. Deciding which colors to mix is a very personal matter, and everyone has their particular favorites.

Five classic colors

There are some colors that have become classics in the Laura Ashley color palette over the past twenty years, appearing in many of the company's paint, wallpaper, and fabric designs. Five of the most popular colors are listed on these two pages, with brief descriptions of how each color came into existence and some of the designs in which it appears. Each color corresponds to one of the color chapters in this book. Shown here are taupe, cowslip, moss, sapphire and rose, and each color has been illustrated with a small color panel to show what it looks like. You will also see these colors illustrated in the color collages on pages 28–37.

Taupe

A pale brown, taupe is one of the neutral colors in the Laura Ashley color palette. It was first introduced as a ground color in the fruit prints such as Blueberry chintz, but has expanded recently into a range of checks, stripes, and plains to suit contemporary styling. *Taupe* is the French word for mole, and it reflects the influence of French style on the collection. When used on its own, taupe needs other neutrals and differing textures to bring it to life and create a very sophisticated look. In floral prints, taupe can be combined with pale pastels, such as in the Melrose drawing room fabric.

By the end of the 1980s, the introduction of cowslip to the Laura Ashley home furnishings collection met the need for a new decorating color. Cowslip brings a contemporary feel to more traditional fabric designs and can be used for a clean, sunny look in older homes as well as in new ones. The Lyme Regis wallpaper in cowslip and the Alba Rose chintz were both very popular. The chintz was a striking floral bouquet spaced on a white ground, and an example of a traditional print being given a modern look by the use of color. Cowslip yellow was also used in the Sweet Pea range of wallpapers and fabrics, and these have the enduring appeal of a country garden in the height of summer.

Cowslip

In recent years, the variety of greens in the collection has been considerably expanded. At first there were four principal greens–dark green, sage, moss, and apple. Of these, moss was the shade that was used most often, both in combination with other colors and by itself. In the mono color prints Sweet Alyssum and Wild Clematis, moss was used with white to create a wonderfully fresh look. It is a true mid-green, a clean green, neither too yellow nor too dark, and is perfect for any room that brings the outdoors into the house, such as a sun porch.

Moss

Sapphire is a very distinctive Laura Ashley color, which is hard to find in the color palettes of other collections. It is as near as you can get to a romantic blue. Sapphire is a pale blue with a hint of lilac, and can look soft and gauzy when mixed with white. Laura Ashley herself decorated a bedroom at her house in France with a sapphire and white print, like a *toile de Jouy*, with white-painted furniture. Slightly deeper tones of sapphire and white can create a fresh, crisp, and clean look. Sapphire works well with other colors such as rose and cowslip, and it suits a variety of climates, adding warmth to rooms in cool climates and looking bright and contemporary in hotter places.

Sapphire

Rose is a classic Laura Ashley color–a soft blue-pink that creates a gentle and romantic room. The shade was chosen by Laura Ashley herself to suit Victorian rose prints without giving too sweet or synthetic an effect, and to sit well with other colors in the collection. For many years, rose pink was the best-selling Laura Ashley color and was an ingredient of many beautiful textile and wallpaper collections, including simple stencil prints such as Cottage Sprig.

Rose

Mixing patterns

It is quite difficult to mix unusual colors successfully by instinct, although some people succeed without knowing why. The answer to successful mixing lies in balancing the elements of hue, tone, and tint to achieve the effect you want. In other words, it is not so much a question of whether blue goes with green, or purple goes with yellow, but the shade of blue with the shade of green, the shade of purple with the shade of yellow, and how much of each you are using in the overall scheme.

You can mix all kinds of patterns together, if you wish, provided you follow a few basic rules, which are similar to those on proportion that were outlined on page 15. If you are going to mix patterns, as a general rule you should choose ones that have similarly sized basic shapes. In other words, mix a small, sprigged floral print with a gingham, or put a big cabbage-rose pattern with wide, bold stripes. The impact will be lost if you combine a tiny flower sprig with large, dramatic stripes because the latter will dominate the former. On the other hand, a small tonal check can look wonderful with a splashy, painterly floral. Placing solid blocks of color somewhere in a scheme of mixed colors will help to unite it and stop it from looking fragmented.

Mixing certain kinds of pattern together–checks and stripes, for example–can work very well but you will probably find that it pays to keep the base color of the fabrics the same, so that there is a consistent link between them. Mixing patterns has become a popular theme in recent years, and you can use the idea in a variety of ways, such as making pillows out of two or three different fabrics (in a simplified version of patchwork), or lining curtains, for example, with a patterned fabric rather than a plain one, or a differing colorway of the same fabric.

There is much to be said for rooms that look as though the contents have been assembled with love and care over a long period rather than decorated in one big shopping spree. The latter may look smart initially, but they also tend to feel impersonal. Some of the early twentieth-century decorators went to considerable lengths to try to create a lived-in, natural look for their clients' newly decorated houses. Nancy Lancaster, of Colefax & Fowler, for example, used to dye new chintz in tea to remove its shiny patina and give the fabric that homely, faded, lived-in look that is the hallmark of English country house style. In recent years there has been a trend towards recycling and renovating existing furniture and fabrics. You can re-use fabrics by cutting them into borders and linings, for example, or pillows. By creating a multi-patterned look, you give yourself an opportunity to incorporate these recycled elements–patches on an armchair or sofa taken from the previous worn covers, adding borders to cornices or curtains, simple patchwork-style pillows or footstools covered in pieces cut from old curtains.

OPPOSITE *This is a singularly beautiful studio. Its arched double-storey window has been given a surprisingly soft and gentle treatment in pastel pinks, straw, and apple greens. Mixing pattern can help to create a sense of vitality, provided the colors are kept to a limited palette. These Laura Ashley fabrics were inspired by the Omega Workshop designs of the Bloomsbury artists Vanessa Bell and Duncan Grant, which can be seen at their home, Charleston in East Sussex, England.*

Juxtapositions of color

Yellow is one of the most invigorating colors in the decorator's palette, and also one of the most versatile. It is used in this Sydney, Australia, living room in a sophisticated scheme with elegant white plasterwork which enhances the sunny, airy feel of the room. The clean lines of the ironwork chairs and the black and white chair covers and rug provide a strong visual contrast with the plain walls.

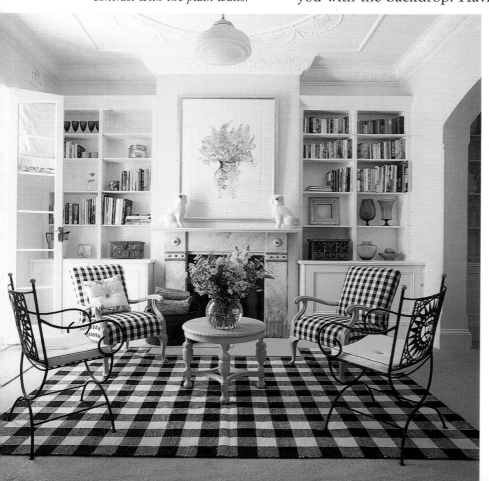

Another important element of color mixing is the way you position the colors to achieve the greatest impact. You can play with color harmonies (colors that complement each other) or with color contrasts (which gain their effect from being opposite each other on the color wheel), and to some extent you can use both together in interior decoration, provided you do so with caution.

It might help if you see your room like a painter's canvas. The bare, undecorated room is the plain, primed canvas that the painter starts with. Some painters begin with a pure white canvas, while others prefer to give the canvas a dark, all-over tone. Using the first scheme, you use the natural lightness of the canvas as a starting point, and you could compare this with a room in which you have painted the walls a light shade of white or a pastel. With the toned canvas, you are starting with a predominantly darker shade, and adding lighter or darker colors to it. Whichever way you start, as with any form of painting, you block in the larger areas of color first, and this is a perfectly sensible approach for decorating a room, too. So, choose your wall and ceiling colors, and your floor color, first. It may be that the room has little natural light and you wish to add to it, in which case you might choose a pale color for the walls and floor. Equally, you may wish to turn the lack of natural light into a decorating virtue, in which case you will keep the scheme deliberately dark and dramatic. Either way, the walls and floors will provide you with the backdrop. Having decided on these two elements, it is time to think about

the next largest item or items–possibly a bed or a sofa, or, if the windows are large, the drapes. Decide, too, where you want the focal point of the room to be, because any large area of strong color will draw the eye to it. If you decide to cover your sofa in crimson, for example, and nothing else in the room is as large or as colorful, all eyes will be focused on the sofa. If you do not want this to happen, the solution is to use equally strong colors on similarly large areas–the curtains, perhaps, or a large rug.

As soon as you add pattern to the color, you change the way it is perceived from a distance. A red and white pattern, for example, when seen from a distance will no longer appear predominantly red but will look pinkish instead. By adding other touches of red, such as red pillows to a red and white checked chair, you concentrate attention on the redness of the red and white pattern.

Adding white cushions will make the pattern appear to be paler and lighter.

Color contrasts can also be used to weaken or strengthen colors–two similarly strong, contrasting colors will more or less cancel each other out. If you use four strong colors, they will each have less impact than if you used just one of these plus white, for example, or a less saturated toning color.

Just as color contrasts play an important part in decorating decisions, so too does tone. Darker or lighter shades of the same color hue can create a very different impression, and you can use tones in a variety of ways to add interest to the scheme, from simply changing the tone of a single color on the walls (see pages 100–1), to shifting the focus in the room by using lighter colors at one end and darker tones at the other, rather like the negative and positive images of a photograph.

You cannot play with color without considering shape, because color and light will draw attention to form. As the Neutrals and Naturals chapter explains, when color is absent, shape and texture become the main focus of interest, but another way of drawing attention to shape is to use a single bright color in a neutral surround. One very bright item in a monochrome scheme will obviously draw attention to that item, and your eye will be drawn to both its color and its form, so this presents you with another means of creating certain key elements in a decorative scheme. An electric-blue vase sitting in a white alcove on a wall, with no other bright colors nearby, will draw the eye, so that the object becomes a major focus of interest. If this item is plain, rather than patterned, the eye will be drawn to its outline against the contrasting background. If it is patterned–such as a Chinese porcelain vase–the pattern itself will become the focus.

There are various small ways in which you can use color to draw attention to shape and form. Piping pillows on a sofa or chair will have the effect of defining the outline and the overall shape of the piece of furniture, and the greater the contrast between the base fabric and the piping, the more obvious this becomes. Small touches like this are a decorator's tricks to channel and focus the eye on the places where you wish it to rest. When they are subtle, they are almost imperceptible, but nevertheless they play a part in the overall success of the scheme and should not be ignored.

A Lloyd Loom chair in eau-de-nil makes a strong statement of shape against the brilliant blue clapboard walls of a porch. Although these colors would not, in all probability, have been planned together, they show that simple shapes and clean colors combine to make an extremely effective decorative statement.

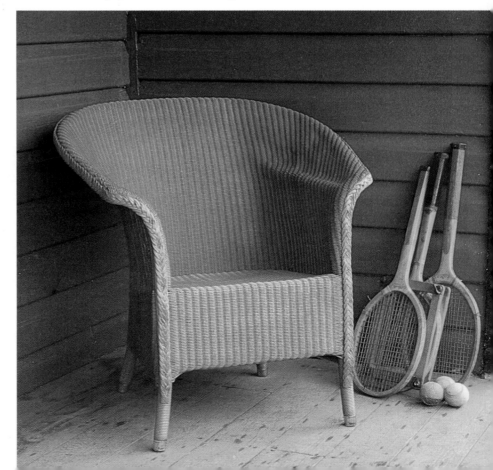

If you are unsure of your abilities in terms of mixing colors, then try to keep the scheme as simple as possible and gradually introduce more detail and pattern when you are sure that the basis is correct. Never add the detail in one area alone. It must be done with a sense of balance–an ability to consider the whole effect.

Practical decorating with color

If you are planning a decorative scheme for any room, it will help you enormously if you take a tip from the professionals and make what they call a storyboard. To all extents and purposes, this is rather like a child's scrapbook. You simply collate the various colored elements in the room–using either actual samples, or blobs of paint or colored pens–on a single sheet of paper. It helps if you try to keep the colored elements in the right ratio to each other–for example, you could make the colored blob for the walls six times the size of the fabric swatch representing the sofa. Represent every colored element, including the trimming and piping, and do not forget the floor. For example, even if it is simply a wood floor you should represent it on the storyboard with a suitably sized blob of similarly colored paint. By putting these elements together, and making any informative notes at the same time, you will find it far easier to plan and pull the scheme together than if you were trying to keep all the ideas in your head.

You will probably find it simplest to compile the storyboard on a very large piece of paper, to fit in all the elements in proportion to one another. You can attach pieces of paper bearing the colored paint blobs to avoid having to redo the storyboard if you change your mind halfway through the scheme.

Compiling a storyboard becomes much easier if you have a good collection of reference material. Keep any magazine articles showing decorative schemes that particularly appeal to you, and have at hand the paint cards produced by manufacturers of good-quality paint who specialize in interesting color ranges.

The color charts

To give you an idea of the different hues and tints of the principal colors discussed in this book, five color charts have been created from a range of fabrics, papers, paints, and natural materials, and include some Laura Ashley designs and colorways. These charts are intended to give a taste of the vast range of shades that are available in each particular color and the variety of possibilities that can be drawn on for inspiration.

As a general rule, the purest color is located in the center of the chart, with the lighter tints above and the darker tones below. If you read across the chart, from left to right, you will see how a color changes, according to what has been mixed with it. In the blue chart, you will find greener blues (those with yellow added to pure blue) on the left, and more mauve blues (those with more red added to the pure blue) on the right. As a result, you can begin to see the subtle differences in hue, tint, and saturation that are contained within a single color theme. Colors appear at their brightest when they are seen at their purest. The pure color is mixed with black for darker shades and with white for paler tints. Each of the charts on the following pages includes different textural elements that illustrate the ways texture can affect the color impact of a hue–from the glossy sheen of a leaf and the silky quality of rose petals, to the natural speckles of oatmeal and the tactile, rough quality of bark.

In the color charts on the following pages, an asterisk indicates a Laura Ashley color.

The most elementary neutral, white, lies in the center of this chart. To the left, the colors become cooler, with silvery grays on the far left, next to greenish neutrals such as ash and bronze. On the right are warmer hues like cream and sand. At the bottom, the darker neutrals range from chocolate brown and rust to charcoal.

Neutrals and naturals

The chart for yellow shows how this color can range from sharp citrus yellows with a high green content on the right, through bright, sunny, primary hues in the center, and the more orangey yellows, with a red content, such as saffron, yellow ocher, turmeric, and orange, on the left.

Yellows

Green is made up of two primary colors, blue and yellow, and the central green in this color chart has a more or less equal balance of these two colors. On the right of the chart are greens with more blue, such as jade and viridian. On the left are those with a strong yellow content, including olive, moss, and apple. Some of the darker greens, like forest and Paris green, are tinted with black to give them a deeper, darker tone.

Greens

In this chart, you can easily see the movement of color from green shades of blue, such as kingfisher and smoke, which are on the left, to red shades of blue, such as sapphire and delphinium, on the right.

Blues

Poppy and scarlet are the primary colors in this chart and sit in the center. To the right are the shades of brick, fresco, terra-cotta, and russet, which contain yellow, ocher, or white. To the left are pinker reds, such as raspberry and deep pink, which are bluer and more purple in nature than the primary hues. The top row shows the softer, pale tones of rose pink, with a high white content, such as crushed strawberry and plaster pink, which contrast with the more vivid pinks below.

Reds

Black and white

Dove gray

Oatmeal

*Ivory

White

Warm gray

Silver

Ash

Pumice

Pale taupe

Slate

Earl Grey

Wainscot

Raw linen

*Taupe

Peat

Charcoal

Bronze

Chocolate

Nut brown

Vanilla

*Stone

String

Oyster

Aran

*Natural

Silver birch

Biscuit

*Cream

*Sand

Desert

Mushroom

Rust

Jute

Nutmeg

Mocha

Fawn

Clay

Bark

Coffee

Almond

Honeydew

*Pale cowslip

*Cowslip

*Cowslip

*Apricot

Naples yellow

*Straw

Butter

Golden hay

Tangerine

Honey

Ginger

Mimosa

Caramel

Orange ocher

Bright orange

Turmeric

Beeswax

Yellow ocher

Butter

Primrose

Powder yellow

Pale gold

Citrus yellow

Buttercup

Lemon

*Old gold

Chamomile

Savannah

Primary yellow

*Deep cowslip

*Old gold

Pale mustard

Orchard yellow

Mustard

Golden rod

Eastern gold

Saffron

Paprika

Tropical green

Apple

*Pale moss

Lichen

Mint

Sage

Grass green

*Moss

Sea green

Emerald

Dark sage

Olive

*Dark moss

Rainforest

Deep emerald green

Spruce

Autumn green

*Aragon green

*Dark green

Malachite

*Pale heath green

Pistachio

*Jade

Pale jade

Aquamarine

*Heath green

*Jade

Turquoise

*Fir green

Seaweed

*Ely green

Rosemary

Bottle green

*Viridian

Deep viridian

Nettle

Racing green

Paris green

Hunting green

Forest

Pale Adam blue

Duck egg

Cloud

Powder blue

Porcelain blue

Adam blue

Azure

Sky blue

Dusty blue

Wedgwood blue

Cerulean blue

*Smoke

Deep powder
blue

Warm smoke

*China blue

Atlantic blue

Kingfisher

*Prussian

Peacock

*Midnight

*Pale chambray

Light cobalt

*Pale sapphire

Lilac

Soft amethyst

Cobalt

*Sapphire

Lavender

Amethyst

*Chambray

Denim

Delphinium

Thistle blue

*Emperor blue

*Classic navy

Purple

Windsor blue

Navy

Indigo

Pale plum

Shell pink

*Rose

Powder pink

*Old rose

*Plum

Deep rose

*Rose pink

*Crushed strawberry

Dusty pink

Mulberry

Raspberry

Magenta

*Crimson

Primary red

Morello

Ruby

Claret

*Burgundy

Scarlet

Soft plaster pink

Pale plaster pink

Pale fresco

Buff

Pale coral

*Deep plaster
pink

*Plaster pink

Coral

Pale terra-cotta

Fresco

Poppy

Pale brick

*Terra-cotta

*Brick

Hot pink

Royal red

Red ocher

*Russet

Brick

Wine

Period colors

You may decide that you wish to decorate your house or flat in colors that were typical of the period in which it was built. Although various august institutions who care for historic houses have done a great deal of research into historical colors, you may find it more practical or harmonious to use colors that are approximate, and suggest the period, rather than those that are absolutely correct. This is true of pattern as well as color. Many of the modern fabric designs are reworkings of designs stored in the world's museums and archives. Sometimes the new design has an updated color theme, colors that have been made less garish and more dusty to represent color before the use of chemical dyes, or a slightly revised pattern. In cases like these, it is the color that will determine whether the fabric is appropriate rather than how close the pattern is to the original. You can read some excellently researched books on the history of interiors, many copiously illustrated with plates of colored drawings that were often produced by the decorators of the period for reference.

How closely you wish to follow any original color scheme or style depends on the architecture of your home as much as anything else. Unfortunately, many houses have been modernized at the expense of the architect's original plans for the building, with period features being lost or replaced by contemporary equivalents. Certain colors predominated in various eras, usually influenced by the materials available, and often by particular trendsetters of the time. All color used in decoration before the Industrial Revolution in the nineteenth century relied on naturally occurring pigments, and the colors popular in different countries were influenced by what was available locally. The names given to the colors, which are still used today, tend to reflect the place of origin of the pigment. For example, burnt sienna, which is a rich, reddish-brown, comes from Siena in Italy, and raw umber, which is a more grayish-brown, comes from Umbria, also in Italy. Those local pigments are likely to influence local color schemes, so you often see houses painted in deep, rich reds where the local earth pigment is red oxide, or in deep yellows where the local pigment is yellow ocher.

Some of the pigments are common to many parts of the world, whereas others are rare and therefore precious. Such colors were often too expensive for domestic use, and eventually cheaper substitutes were found. The rich, deep colors of the Renaissance period—the golds, lapis lazuli, cobalt blues, ruby reds, deep greens, and porphyry greens—relied on some of the more expensive pigments. Heavy hangings, velvets, and weighty furniture characterized the style, as any glance around a gallery of Renaissance paintings will show. With the turn of the seventeenth century, the style and color palette lightened and changed. Baroque and rococo, with their emphasis on swirling movement

OPPOSITE *Walls painted in toning blue and bluish-green give a wonderful feeling of translucency and depth. Texture becomes extremely important when you use subtle, simple color combinations, and the figured silk of the elegant sofa and chairs, and the thick pile of the carpet, are thrown into relief in this eighteenth-century room at Mount Vernon, Virginia. It is the family home of George Washington, and has been furnished and decorated exactly as it would have been when Washington was alive.*

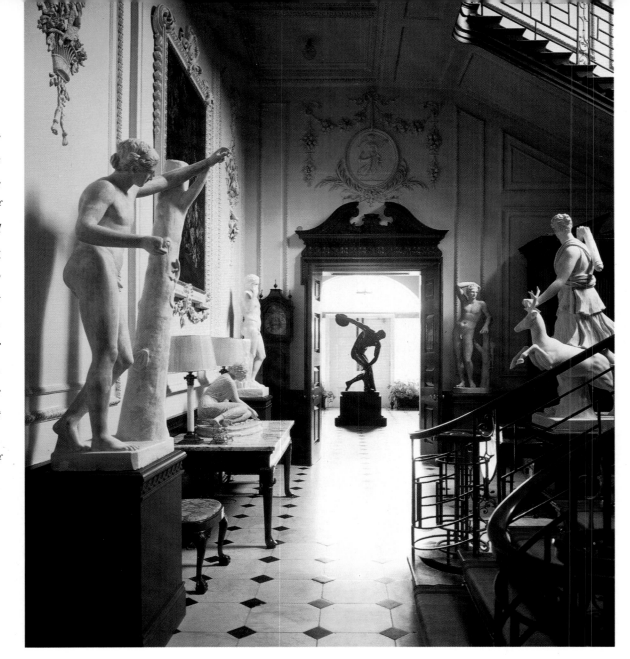

The yellow and white Staircase Hall at Hatchlands in Surrey is a classic example of the early work of the architect Robert Adam. If you wish to display any kind of sculpture, you need a setting which allows attention to focus on its form. Neutrals schemes—here, yellow, white, black, and brown—are ideal for this purpose since they recede, allowing the artifacts to take pride of place. Note how the light catches the texture of the statues, making a wonderful play of shadow and enhancing the form.

and light colors, introduced a whole new era in the color palette for the interior, with the use of pastel shades of pink, blue, pale green, gold, and white.

By the mid-eighteenth century, the color palette, although still light, became more prolific, thanks to the work of Robert Adam, the renowned Scottish architect. Adam, having taken the Grand Tour in the 1750s, brought back the sunshine colors from Italy, and his color schemes, richly adorned with stucco work, were in mid-tones of green, blue and violet, with white, and sometimes gold, as relief. With the revival of Classicism, this lightheartedness went and a more drab and formal decorating style intervened. The emphasis of the Palladian revival was on form rather than on ornamentation, and a duller color palette ensured that the classical lines were emphasized. Drab—a particularly dull greeny-brown—was one of the colors, often offset with putty color, white, or pale gray.

Fabrics

The range of fabrics at your disposal is so extensive that you can feel spoiled for choice. However, there are a few rules worth noting. If possible, start with a relatively clear idea of what you are looking for–the color, type of pattern, or atmosphere of your finished room may be enough to set you on the right track. Try not to spend too long gazing at pattern samples at any one time, otherwise your eye may become confused. If possible, choose times for browsing around stores when they are not full of busy shoppers who may jostle or distract you, when they are not about to close for the night, and when the staff will be available to give you their attention and advice.

Try to ensure you have a clear idea of the weight and texture of the fabric that you need, such as an upholstery weight for soft furnishings. Having chosen the fabric, keep a swatch in your notebook so that you can refer to it when choosing other decorative elements such as braids, piping, or cushions. Color-matching different fabrics and trimmings by memory alone is at best hit-and-miss and, at worst, disastrous and a waste of money.

Fabric weights and finishes come in a vast range these days, but you need to choose one that is suitable for the purpose you have in mind. Today, most fabrics are graded, as they are in the Laura Ashley range, by function–for drape; for drape and upholstery; for upholstery; for sheers; and for linings. You can, of course, ignore these gradings, but if so you will have to be careful because there are always sound reasons why the fabrics have been so categorized. You can use lining fabrics as top fabrics, if you wish, or use top fabrics as linings, provided they are roughly the same weight. Mattress ticking, now frequently used as a top fabric, was once deemed suitable only as a functional fabric. You can also create your own fabrics by stitching and piecing them together to make borders, stripes, and even patchworks of pattern and color.

Sage green, yellow ocher, and Indian red are all tints of purer colors to which black has been added, so that they appear less demanding and more subtle. Because they have roughly the same tonal values, they tend to cancel each other out, creating a scheme that is more neutral in feel than a description of the colors involved would lead you to suspect.

Paint There is an increasingly good range of paints on the market, many of them manufactured by specialists in their field. Although they cost slightly more than most paints, they have the advantage of a more subtle range of colors and a limited color palette. This may sound like a contradiction in terms, but just as too many fabrics can confuse your eye for pattern and color, so extensive paint charts can create a form of blindness–you may feel unable to make a choice and in a panic you could opt for something unsuitable or disappointing.

With paint, it is not only the question of choosing the right shade–you need also to find an appropriate paint for the task in hand. There are various paint compositions available, which are determined by the ingredients used. Originally, paint was basically pigment and chalk turned into a paste-like solution, with water or oil as the binding agent. With the mechanization of the paint industry during the Industrial Revolution and subsequent advances in the chemical industry, paints have become increasingly sophisticated and varied. You are now offered an almost infinite range of types of paints–including latex, gloss paints, floor paints, and outdoor paints, all in a variety of finishes–and a whole new range of paint-like substances, in the form of woodstains, have recently come on the market. You therefore have to consider what you want to paint, and the best medium to use for the job in hand. Paints

Adam green was one of the most popular decorating colors in the eighteenth century. It lends itself marvelously to displays of wooden furniture and paintings, which perhaps explains why it has long been popular as a decorating color for large country houses. Here, at Homewood House in Baltimore, the color has been deepened to varying shades of apple green, while keeping the overall Adam style. White plasterwork, another classic Adam feature, helps to define and focus attention on the architecture.

available from good-quality manufacturers, and particularly from traditional paint manufacturers, are increasingly including old-fashioned finishes, such as distemper and flat oil paint. Originally, distemper contained lime to help prevent mold spores from forming–a necessity in those days and one of the reasons why pantries were often distempered. Unlike modern latex paint, distemper allows the natural stone, brick, or plaster it covers to "breathe," allowing moisture through. Modern latex paint, when applied to a damp surface, will bubble and crack.

Paint, until recently, was largely only applied to walls, ceilings, doors, and window frames, as well as kitchen cupboards. As the pine furniture that proliferated in many homes across several continents began to need a facelift, so painted furniture has become increasingly popular. Paint finishes of various sorts have given most amateur interior decorators a chance to revitalize their homes in imaginative and original ways without spending a fortune, so it is hardly surprising that these paint effects have become a major decorating story in the 1980s and 1990s.

Wood, as opposed to plaster, can be painted in a variety of finishes, depending on whether you want the natural appearance of the wood to show through, or whether you wish to disguise it. Durability of finish is also a key point, and it often pays to varnish a paint effect, whether for furniture or for walls, to make it last longer.

Wallpaper

As with paints and fabrics, there are different types and weights of wallpapers available, designed for different purposes. Laura Ashley produces three different kinds–embossed papers, which have a relief pattern and plain finish and can be painted to suit your color scheme; standard wallpapers, which are plain or printed; and vinyl and matt vinyl papers, which have been coated to make them fully washable, and are suitable for any rooms where steam may affect the paper. Borders and friezes are also available, in varying widths, which can be used by themselves or with other wallpapers.

Before wallpaper came into general use with the arrival of the Industrial Revolution, which mechanized the production process, wallpaper was hand-printed, using wooden blocks, and supplied in squares or small strips. The amount of time involved in its manufacture meant it was only available to the very rich. Some manufacturing houses still supply hand-blocked papers today, but at a price. There is nothing quite like the beauty and quality of a good hand-blocked paper, but unfortunately it is very expensive. However, many companies, including Laura Ashley, can print wallpaper designs so that they resemble hand-blocked designs.

Mixing colors successfully

Although it is relatively easy to devise an interior decoration scheme using a very limited color palette, mixing several colors together can present problems for the inexperienced home decorator because the scheme can lack unity and cohesion. The secret of successfully mixing several colors lies in choosing some large areas of plain color, and clever mixing of tones of the same hue. In fact, the choice of tone of each color–whether light or dark–has a very important part to play in the overall mood and atmosphere of the room.

In this deliberately constructed room set, the starting point is a palette of four "bright" colors representing more or less similar mid-tones–pink, yellow, turquoise, and apple green. If you do not understand what "tone" means, screw up your eyes when you look at the photographs. Certain colors will appear lighter than others–this is what is meant by tone. It is easy to confuse tone with brightness of color, but colors that appear bright are not always light. It is much easier to learn about the differences between tone and brightness when looking at plain colors. As soon as other colors are included, your eye is distracted and you fail to notice whether the effect is predominantly light or dark. White added to a pattern will automatically jump out at you, and may cause you to think that the overall effect is lighter than it really is, but if you half-close your eyes when you look at it again, the true tonal value of the scheme will emerge.

The colors in this room were chosen from swatches of fabric set against an expanse of yellow paper to represent the wall color. It is crucial to begin your scheme by trying different swatches of fabric next to one another to see how they work. At the swatch stage, it is important to look at print as well as color. In this room, a floral linen has been chosen for the curtains. The sand-colored background is important because it is a mid-tone and therefore works with both the pale and dark schemes of this room which are shown on the following pages. The pink and turquoise upholstery colors pick out the pink and turquoise flower colors in the print. A turquoise linen border has been sewn around the edge of the curtains to give them definition against the yellow wall.

Understanding the difference between tone and brightness of color is important because it affects the way the colors "read" from a distance: dark colors seem to recede and light colors appear to advance. To make matters more difficult for you, reds look as if they are nearer than they really are and blues look further away. Balancing these factors of light and dark, and advancing and receding colors, is an important step in learning to manipulate them to achieve the effects you want, and in creating a look that is warm or cool. Colors with red and yellow in them are perceived as warm; colors containing blue and green are perceived as cool.

Here, the four principal colors have been used for the major items in the room, using the mid-tones of pink, turquoise, and apple green for the sofas and chair, and yellow for the walls. Because the tonal values of each of these items are fairly similar, the colors balance. A shocking pink sofa, with bottle green and royal blue armchairs, would have concentrated attention on the pink sofa to the exclusion of the other two colors. You can therefore use color choices to manipulate the effect you are trying to achieve.

In this photograph, curtains have been added to the basic room to unify the scheme. The sand-colored linen curtains with their turquoise and pink floral pattern complement the mid-tone background and the turquoise and pink sofas.

45

Touches of lighter tones have now been added to the basic scheme in the form of smaller accessories, such as cushions in pale tones of the three main colors (pale pink, pale mint green, and pale sky blue), throws, and pale painted furniture. The overall effect is much more open and increases the feeling of space in the room. You can use this to great effect to make a small or cramped room appear larger than it is. A much paler tone on the walls would further increase the appearance of space.

In the same basic room, light accessories have been replaced with a variety of dark ones: predominantly, a selection of plain, dark cushions in deep bottle green, navy blue, deep maroon, plum, and rich raspberry red; a dark burgundy carpet; various throws on the sofa; a dark-toned large oil painting on the wall; and dark wood furniture. The effect is to deepen and enclose the space, pulling the sofas and chairs apparently closer together, and giving the room a much greater solidity.

The way we perceive color depends in part on where and how it is positioned, and the colors which are put next to it. In these two photographs, differently toned cushions have been added to the green armchair, to show how they affect its base color. Here, the base fabric looks darker, because the light cushions make the plain green fabric of the sofa deepen and appear to recede.

In this photograph, two deeper-toned cushions in denim and forest green have been added to the green armchair. They lighten the color of the fabric, and make it appear to come forward.

On this page, the pink sofa has been given three treatments. ABOVE LEFT *It has been given pale-toned pillows in pink and white gingham, cowslip, and mint. The white in the gingham appears to come toward you.* ABOVE RIGHT *The sofa with dark-toned pillows in deep bottle green and dark maroon. They enrich and deepen the pink fabric of the sofa.* LEFT *A striped throw and a mixture of light and dark pillows have been added. The yellow on the front of the embroidered pillow makes it appear to advance toward you.*

OPPOSITE *The same exercise has been carried out on the turquoise sofa, but pattern has also been introduced.* TOP LEFT *Pillows in pale pink, eau-de-nil, and a large check have been added.* TOP RIGHT *The throw intensifies the colors in the cushions and creates a feeling of harmony.* BOTTOM LEFT *The effect in these photographs of the turquoise sofa is more muted as the contrast between light and dark decreases.* BOTTOM RIGHT *The pattern of the throw links the extremes of light and dark tones, and creates a more harmonious overall effect.*

neutrals and naturals

The overall effect of using neutrals in decorating is to create a feeling of space, tranquility and harmony. If you do not want an interior that might date quickly, then a neutrals scheme is almost always the sensible option. This is in part because it has been popular at so many points in the history of architecture and interior decoration—most memorably, perhaps, in the stucco and plasterwork of the Adam brothers in the eighteenth century—and in part because it enhances any architectural details, so it never truly goes out of vogue in decorating schemes.

Although white is not strictly a color, it is one of the most important elements in any decorative scheme, providing either the entire basis for it, or areas of contrast in any number of different color combinations. A very large portion of the range of neutrals lies in the white, cream, and beige sector, while ivories, taupes, sands, stones, jutes, browns and grays are considered to be natural colors, because they are found in natural objects and settings.

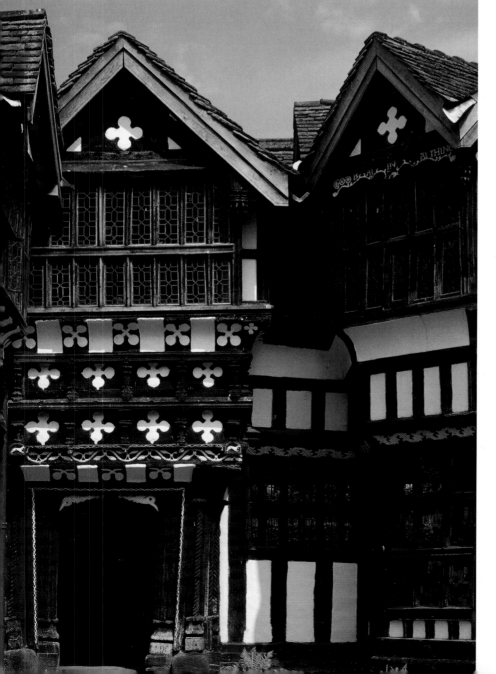

Remember when using white that it has many shades. It is not the simple, flat color you first imagine; and the composition of the fabric, paint, plaster, paper, or wood will determine the way that it reflects light, and whether as a consequence it looks warm or cold. You can play with different tones of white, making subtle shading distinctions, to create the kind of shadow that you would automatically obtain from architectural relief. This is a particularly valuable technique when you need to create some definition and interest that would not otherwise exist on a wall, perhaps because it has no architectural features or interest of its own.

Little Moreton Hall in Cheshire, England, is considered to be the most perfect example of a timber-framed manor house anywhere in the United Kingdom. The black timbers and white-painted panels form a striking contrast and prove that a neutrals scheme can be equally as dramatic as one using bold colors.

It is no accident that picture or sculpture galleries are often designed with white walls and pale floors. These provide the perfect foil to show off decorative elements, be they furniture, fabrics, paintings, or even people. Neutrals have been a major feature in many specific decorating styles: in the pale ice-cream colors of the stucco of London's terraced houses by Nash; in the spacious interiors inspired by Minimalism with its bleached floors and furniture, and white-painted walls; in the bluish-white-painted surfaces of Scandinavian style; or the simple, white-painted stone houses of the Mediterranean countries, where the reflectivity of white helps to reduce the heat by deflecting it.

Neutrals schemes rely much more on clever use of light and texture than any other color scheme. Pale colors, whites, and creams are highly reflective, so they bounce natural light off the walls and back into the room to create an airy atmosphere. The textures in the room are also enhanced because the lack of color automatically makes you focus on the surface of objects. A combination of the two elements is the hallmark of any neutrals scheme, be it the simple, flat expanses of white-painted stone, the cool marble floors, and the white cotton dustsheets of an Italianate interior, or the jutes and hemps, linens, canvases, and pale, bleached wood of more modern interiors. You could, very successfully, decorate a whole house with neutrals, from pale dove gray through to ocher, varying them slightly in each room, to give a subtle but wonderfully rich and textural effect that links the rooms in a harmonious theme. Whatever the look you choose, it is important to ensure it stays in character.

Light plays an essential part in any neutrals scheme, whether natural light from large windows or deliberately angled artificial lighting, since it is the play of shadows on these monochromatic surfaces that creates the real interest and atmosphere of each room. Any room in the house, from bathroom to kitchen, can be decorated with neutrals and naturals, but it is important to use the room's existing features as the cornerstone of the scheme. An historic house with dark oak beams, for example, would require a very different treatment from a barn conversion with stripped pine or elm floors. In the former, natural, soft, thick fabrics like jacquards, chenilles, crewelwork, and damasks could be good choices, while in the latter you might opt for harder textures such as canvases, sailcloths, and cotton reps, which are more in keeping with the sharper, cleaner lines of the architecture. The artifacts–whether roughly hewn stone jars, simple Wedgwood creamware, or delicate handblown glass–will also help to set the theme and tone, and should be selected for their ability to harmonize with both the setting and the other furnishing elements. Ensuring this continuity of texture, tone, and form is the key to successful decorating in neutrals and naturals.

The influence of neutrals

Neutrals have long been used in decorative schemes, and they featured heavily in the designs of the Georgians, such as Robert Adam and John Nash, as well as later designers such as those in the Arts and Crafts movement, which was particularly influential in its use of natural colors and unpolished wood. Simple domestic interiors of the past also used a lot of white because it was inexpensive, bright and easy to keep clean.

The ornate, richly colored, and heavy decorative schemes of the Victorians and Edwardians, and the vivid color schemes of the Roaring Twenties, were met by an inevitable backlash in the 1930s, when neutrals became the height of fashion. This was also the heyday of the interior decorator. Prior to this, architects, cabinet-makers, curtain-makers, and upholsterers had provided the only real guidance on interior design, in a rather piecemeal fashion. After World War I, however, the new-found emancipation of women led them to look for suitable work, and many well-to-do women found their niche in advising on the arrangement of interiors.

Although now chiefly recognized as an architect and designer of furniture, it was as an interior designer that Charles Rennie Mackintosh was best known in his lifetime (1868–1928). He employed contrasts of light and dark, in monochromatic schemes, to create an almost Japanese-like simplicity in his designs, with their consequent emphasis on form and structure. In the drawing room at Mackintosh's own house at 120 Mains Street, in his native Glasgow, Scotland, he created dramatic and stark effects with just this emphasis, using white for the walls, floors, and most of the furniture. The only soft element in the room came from the see-through muslin drapes over the windows–a style that has found favor again today nearly one hundred years later.

Mackintosh was the exponent, *par excellence*, of monochromatic effects in decoration, and it is largely thanks to his original influence that a range of black and white inspired schemes became the vogue in the Jazz Age of the 1930s. Black and white is still a popular decorative emblem today, particularly for hallways and kitchens, because it is an excellent way to show off decorative motifs or geometric patterns. Black and white tiled floors have long been popular in grand entrances, and black and white tiling was frequently used in newly constructed 1930s bathrooms, with plain white bathroom fittings. Today, the effect is often softened by the addition of natural wood surfaces, replacing the chrome and glass popular in the 1930s, to create a warmer, more sympathetic, but still elegant finish.

The decorative style of Syrie Maugham (1879–1955) was a natural extension of some of the principles that underpinned Charles Rennie Mackintosh's interiors. The former wife of Henry Wellcome, head of the pharmaceutical firm, and latterly married to the novelist Somerset Maugham, she became a decorator, having worked in the antiques department of the prestigious London shop Fortnum & Mason. Her hallmark as a decorator was her penchant for light-colored fabrics, and for stripping furniture of its previous dark stains, then either painting or waxing it to restore its original, natural, pale wood luster–described at the time as "pickling."

The all-white interior which Syrie Maugham created in her London house in 1927 took this neutrals theme a stage further, but departed from the spare, sculptural lines of Charles Rennie Mackintosh. She blended ornate French Louis XIV furniture, which she stripped and waxed, or painted in pale colors, with the then popular Modernist chrome and glass, setting off the uncompromising lines of modern furniture with generous swathes of plain but textured neutral fabrics. This created an eclectic mix that neatly summed up this period of massive social upheaval following the end of World War I

The use of tones of cream, beige, and white has recently found favor again in interior decoration, and has become a popular idiom in 1990s style. This is in part because these tones provide a necessary contrast with the bold colors and patterns popular in the 1980s; partly because there is growing interest in the 1990s in conservation, restoration, and a more natural way of life; and also because of the growing popularity of the bleached Scandinavian look and of softer colors faded by the sun.

The sharper monochromatic schemes of the 1930s, with their distinct contrasts of black and white, have given way recently to much more subtle decorative schemes of gray, white, and taupe, where the interplay of light and shadow lends an almost architectural feel to the overall color scheme. Soft textures and non-reflective surfaces are very much a part of this kind of look.

Monochromatic color schemes, in this case in black, gray, and white, can be extremely effective, as the Great Hall at Syon House, England, designed by Robert Adam in the 1760s, demonstrates. Spare, elegant, and cool, monochromatic schemes are ideal for large, light rooms.

Style

Although predominantly white, this room benefits enormously from the touches of ocher in the warm color of the wooden boards, the large print on the wall, and pieces of occasional furniture. Without any strong color to distract the eye, the focus is drawn to the shapes of the furniture–a nicely balanced mix of hard and soft lines.

As soon as you eschew bold color, you force the eye to concentrate on the two other key aspects of interior design: shape and texture. If you are opting for a neutrals-inspired scheme, then you are, perforce, going to draw attention to these factors, and it becomes an essential part of the style to make the most of them, whether in the form of furniture, textiles, or architecture.

A neutrals scheme will draw attention to the shape of both the architecture and the furniture, since the eye is not distracted by color. If you have particularly good furniture, or a handsomely proportioned room, for example, a neutrals scheme may well be the best option. You can create the odd splash of color in a predominantly neutrals room, which will help to bring it to life and give it focus. Clever positioning of the furniture becomes particularly important and, in this kind of scheme, the best solution can be to opt for less rather than more, keeping the attention on a few attractive pieces. This is a look that is strictly for those who like clean lines and spacious rooms.

However, there are many other neutrals schemes to choose from. You can create a minimal look with white walls, pale woods, and white fabrics, or you can opt for an eclectic and cluttered look, with pale walls forming the background to a magpie-like jumble of books, magazines, pictures, and plants. If you have an interesting combination of pieces of furniture, you may find that they look most striking and effective when set against a neutral background. For a serene and elegant room, you could use soft tones of creams, buttermilks, or pale grays, perhaps with accents of naturals such as soft smoky blue or earthy terra-cotta. You can also choose other looks: rustic simplicity, with coir matting, terra-cotta tiles, and country furniture; high sophistication, with white walls, details picked out in black, metal curtain poles, modern furniture and abstract lines; or supreme elegance, with decorative wallpapers, richly textured fabrics, and beautiful trimmings and details. Cherished collections of objects add style, emphasis, and individuality to a neutrals room, whether they are assortments of china, photographs, pictures, or other collectibles.

Texture is a valuable element of any decorative scheme but it has a particular relevance when neutrals are involved since, in the absence of color and pattern, the eye tends to be drawn to the texture. You can therefore begin to consider different kinds of texture, from hard, hairy, tweedy, or nubbly on the one hand to soft, smooth, silky, or lacy on the other. Ideally, try to contrast different textures, such as the rough, tough consistency of jute, in the form of sisal rugs, with the smooth, polished pale wood on which they might lie. Or you could contrast the translucency and smoothness of glass with the texture of a white-painted brick wall, perhaps. Large pebbles, washed smooth by the tide over thousands of years, make a wonderful contrast with the pale distempered surface of rough plaster in a window recess. A collection of old bottles can sit on a roughly hewn wooden shelf. Lace panels can be sewn onto pillows, to create a welcome textural relief from the heavier, denser weaves of upholstery fabrics. These differences in texture bring interiors to life and although the effect is subtle, it is also extremely effective.

Texture

Texture is, quite often, the last element to be considered but it can make all the difference to the success, or otherwise, of any scheme. Combinations of textures that do not go together, or are too similar can create a disturbing atmosphere. Interiors that were popular in the 1950s, with all-pervasive smooth surfaces of plastic and glass, were sometimes cold and unfriendly to the point of alienation, particularly when combined with colors created from strong chemical dyes.

A neutral decor today is synonymous with a natural look. It is the textural contrasts that create this look, by copying the diversity of texture found in nature itself. Among the different textures available to the interior decorator, wood is one of the most rewarding surfaces of all. It introduces a considerable wealth of color, texture, and pattern to a room before any other element is added, and it also has warmth and character. The easiest and most common way to use wood in a neutrals room is through the furniture, which can range from elegant Federal or heavy Victorian to French country, painted Swedish, or practical domestic furniture.

Many hardwoods, from which most furniture is made, have rich surface patterning and sometimes color variation as well, from the intricately swirling patterns of walnut to the smooth simplicity and fine grain of beech or chestnut. Each wood has its own color, from the deep reddish-brown of rosewood or mahogany to the golden yellow of maple. Part of a cabinet-maker's skill lies in creating designs that make the most of the wood's grain, texture, and color, and also in choosing a wood that suits the purpose for which it is intended. Expensive pieces of furniture are usually made from hardwoods and fruitwoods, perhaps with decorative veneers or inlays, while country furniture, such as dining tables and dressers, is often made from pine, which is an inexpensive softwood. Until relatively recent times, softwoods were always painted.

Many of the untreated woods, such as pine, chestnut, elm, and beech, are fairly pale in their own right, but will darken with age indoors if not preserved in some way. To create paler wood surfaces without losing the character of the wood itself, you can opt for one of the white woodstains, which have now become very sophisticated in terms of both the products themselves and the range of colors they are supplied in. Many of them are water-based, which allows you to tint the wood with a flat, opaque finish that still permits the grain of the wood to show through. Alternatively, you can use pickling wax or wash the wood in white paint which you then partly wipe off for an antiqued effect.

Paints

The formulation of paint varies according to the manufacturer so, when planning a neutrals-based scheme, think carefully about the paint, since the sheen or lack of it will be crucially important in the final look. An old-fashioned distemper (which is based on lime), will give a completely different look from a latex velvet, particularly when there is no other color around to distract the eye from the paint's finish.

Traditional paint formulations have a long local history, with the formula, and sometimes the color, varying according to the pigments and minerals available. For example, the traditional stone houses of Wales and Greece, although very different in character, are painted in limewash. This is an excellent paint to use for stone walls because, being porous, it allows the stone to "breathe." The resulting paint is powdery and thin, therefore allowing the underlying texture of the walls to show through.

Limewash is usually a simple mixture with no color added, although pigments, particularly natural earth ones such as yellow ocher or burnt umber, can be added to it.

Magnolia and gardenia, both shades of off-white, are two of the biggest-selling paint colors. This is because they are easy to live with and provide a good background for many different decorating and furniture styles. In addition, many people like them because they are warmer than pure white, which is very cold. However, the range of paints in neutral tones has expanded considerably in the last few years and there are now many more subtle options open to anyone wishing to decorate in neutrals.

As with colors, the bluer tones of white will seem colder, and the yellow or pink tones much warmer. If you find you have made the wrong choice, you can do a great deal to warm up a cool color by altering the lighting. You can choose from halogen, fluorescent, daylight-effect, low-wattage, and tinted bulbs, or atmospheric groups of candles, to create a variety of moods in a room and to soften or warm the decorative scheme, according to the effect you want to create.

This close-up of a pantry reveals the real joy of neutrals—the important role of texture, from the rough wicker of the basket to the smooth surface of the eggs, the translucent sheen of the glass jars, and the almost papery texture of the vegetables. Light and shadow play a major role in creating this feeling of texture, and subtly different shades of color—as shown in the toning cream paintwork—enhance it.

59

Papers

If you want a pattern, design, motif, or texture on your walls, then paper is an excellent choice. The texture plays an important part in the overall look, whether you are using a thick, embossed paper or thin lining paper. There is a wealth of wallpaper designs that are more or less self-colored, with only a small tonal variation between the pattern and the backing color. If you find areas of plain paper or paint too stark, this type of paper would be an obvious choice. Self-stripes in cream and white look sophisticated without appearing cold in any way, and are suitable for most situations. Monotone wallpapers are tonal with simple designs, which give walls an interesting textural quality in subtle, neutral tones without overwhelming a room. Equally, large-print wallpapers which represent the designs of tonal damask fabrics are an ideal way to introduce pattern and decoration into a neutrals color scheme, and are especially suitable for elegant and formal rooms. Geometric patterns or stripes tend to suit the modern idiom better than more ornate designs, although much depends on the architecture of the room and the style of the furnishings.

Fabrics

With fabric, texture really comes into its own. There is a rich and exciting variety of weaves, patterns, and materials from which to choose, from heavy raised brocades to gossamer- thin voiles, from roughly woven tweeds to shimmery silks. The use of one color makes the texture of the fabric its most outstanding quality, and much depends on the fibers used in its construction, as well as in the weight and sheen of the cloth. Among the fabrics suitable for neutrals schemes are those with a self-pattern, such as jacquards (which can have complex self-patterns) and dobbies (which have simple, geometric self-patterns). Epinglés, which are similar in texture to tapestry but have looser stitches, are ideal fabrics for neutrals schemes. Natural, unbleached linens are also extremely effective, as are pale florals that look as though they have been gently faded by the sun.

Fortunately for the home decorator, many of the simple neutral fabrics are inexpensive, because they are the unadorned, unrefined basic cloth. Muslin is an example of this, with its tough, heavy-duty, matte character. It is one of the most popular natural, unbleached fabrics, and is particularly suitable for summer decorating, as it can be used to make slip-covers for upholstered furniture that would otherwise look too hot in the summer. These covers can be removed when the weather starts to get cooler in the autumn. Originally used for lining grander fabrics, muslin's serviceable qualities and sheer value for money have made it popular for a range of soft furnishings, particularly for the more architecturally inspired types of shades, such as roller or Roman shades, and for simple, generously draped and dressed curtains. Entire rooms have been decorated in muslin, with draped bedheadings, swagged and dressed draperies, and simply designed chair covers. Combined with other neutral fabrics such as crisp white bedlinen and sisal rugs, muslin creates a look that is both luxurious yet simple. One of the advantages of using a plain, neutral, and inexpensive fabric such as this is that you can afford to buy enough of it to drape it extravagantly.

Other good choices for fabrics in a neutrals scheme are those with a strongly textured weave, such as linens, cotton reps, and rich jacquard patterns in silk or wool, and loosely woven woolens and cottons. Slubby silks, like textured noil and tusser, react with the light to create marvelous patterns of highlight and shade. Linen union, a mixture of cotton and linen, makes an extremely tough fabric that is ideal for either upholstery or drapery, and comes in some wonderful, rich, neutral, and natural colors, with interesting self-woven patterns or printed designs. Printed cottons and silks, in monochromatic color combinations–grays, whites, beiges, and blacks–also fit in well in this kind of interior, as do embroidered cottons in pale colors and simple ginghams for a Scandinavian look. One of the recent innovations is the introduction of crewelwork-style machine-embroidered fabrics, often in white or cream on a beige or pastel background. Large rooms can take more elaborate fabric patterns, and the use of drapery in

Texture plays an important role in this neutrals color scheme, as does the mixture of delicately patterned fabrics. From the translucent folds of the curtain to the polished sheen of the boards and the rough surface of the woven jacquard used for some of the sofa and chair covers, texture helps to create visual interest in what would otherwise be a uniform color scheme.

abundance will allow you more freedom with pattern, but beware of choosing patterns that are too bright and bold for the size of the room, as they will be overwhelming.

Translucent fabrics–in the form of lace and voiles in whites, creams, and beiges–are always popular, in particular for drapes, either set at the window or around a bed. The soft, sweeping lines of these fabrics give a room a romantic and sometimes mysterious atmosphere. Sheer muslins, voiles, machine-made lace, and fine silks have been employed for years as under-curtains or glass-curtains, hung on simple rods next to the window behind more ornate draperies. Today they are often used independently as bed hangings, particularly in hot climates where they serve a very important function as mosquito netting. These fine fabrics sometimes look nice when contrasted with a heavier and more elaborate fabric, such as heavily patterned cotton, silk damask, or linen, to give a rich, vibrant quality to the room.

Windows

Neutral color schemes work very well for most windows, since they allow the attention to concentrate on the window itself. They are, therefore, best used to frame an already distinguished-looking window, in the same way that a picture frame can set off a painting. According to the style of the window and the feel of the room, the window dressing can be simple and unobtrusive or elaborate and decorative. Details which would not be seen on highly patterned fabrics can be used to great advantage on curtains and drapes in neutrals color schemes. For example, draperies in a neutrals room with a contemporary feel could be given pinch pleats or a simple tab heading, while those in a period room could be given swags and cascades, or perhaps a cornice cut into harlequin points or scallops. Trimmings are also very important in neutrals schemes, because they add depth, interest, detail, and texture–you could arrange toning braids across the curtain headings, tie back the curtains with thick loops of cord, or perhaps pipe the leading edge of each curtain in a different pattern or color. You can also create interest by stitching together strips of contrasting fabrics to make striped curtains.

Windows with handsome proportions, such as the elegant tall windows you often find in historic houses, are often best left unadorned except for simple wooden shutters or perhaps a plain shade in stiff canvas. Alternatively, Roman shades in plain muslin or London shades–which have a simple drawstring mechanism–in a fine, plain white cotton weave fit neatly into any window that is taller than it is wide, and offset the proportions well. Roller or Roman shades in wide, short windows can look wrong.

One of the other popular uses for neutral fabrics has been for translucent window-screens. Lace has traditionally been used for this purpose, and there are many new and exciting ways to tackle the problem of privacy in a town house or apartment without resorting to machine-made synthetic glass curtains. If you choose carefully, the window-screen becomes a stylish statement in its own right. Organdy–a form of crisp, stiff, muslin–can be used, hanging plain and unpleated from a simple pole, or a translucent version of the London shade can be constructed instead. Alternatively, antique pieces of lace can be draped over a pole so that they hang in folds.

When planning the furniture for a neutrals scheme, you need to think carefully about shape as well as color and texture. For most neutrals schemes, the emphasis is on space and light, so you need to ensure that the overall effect does not look cluttered. Large sofas and deep chairs, upholstered in pale, textured fabrics, look good combined with painted or stripped and waxed woods. You can create a wonderfully informal and relaxed mood by using furniture made from rattan, wicker, and cane, or choosing Lloyd Loom chairs, sofas, or low tables, especially if you combine them with plenty of plants. Sometimes, if the atmosphere and style of the room are appropriate, decorative elements such as pictures may look best if kept large and simply framed. If you opt for strong color in the form of paintings or posters, check that they make a sufficient statement to warrant the intrusion of the color, either by hanging them in close proximity to one another or repeating their colors and shapes elsewhere. Failure to do so will result in the painting or poster dominating the room, which may of course be your intention, especially if the painting is the focus for the entire room. Alternatively, if you do not want to introduce large splashes of color, you can decorate the walls with an eclectic mix of small watercolors, engravings, antique maps, or black and white photographs.

Flowers, too, need to be considered in this kind of setting. Massed displays of sculptural flowers in a single color will enhance the neutrals theme of the room–big bowls of white or yellow tulips, perhaps, a large jug of white or pale blue hydrangeas, or a silver rose bowl filled with white or pale pink roses. A simple display of different colored flowers might be ideal for an informal room decorated in neutral or natural colors and filled with country furniture. Architectural houseplants, such as spiky palms, suit a sophisticated neutrals room and accentuate its clean lines, or you might wish to soften the atmosphere with huge pots of marguerites or frilly-leafed scented geraniums.

A neutrals scheme is excellent for displaying sculpture of almost any sort, enabling you to focus attention properly on the shape and texture of the piece. Whether your taste is for representational or abstract forms, positioning the sculpture carefully against a plain, unadorned background will make the most of it.

Furniture and finishes

A Cream Kitchen

A neutrals and naturals theme was chosen for this large, light kitchen, in which the warm, glowing tones of wood are the major feature, for the floors, the kitchen cupboards, and the work surfaces. It illustrates the point that when you remove color from a decorating scheme, your eye automatically focuses on shape and texture. You notice, for example, the different colors in the wood itself, and the way that the grain runs. Details become important, and your eye is drawn to anything that stands out–be it the little painted pie safe, or the thick, soft folds of the burlap shade at the window–in which texture and shape instead of color play a major feature. The old wood beam above the window, with its irregular form, stands out both tonally and architecturally from the smoothness of the rest of the room, and its roughly hewn shape is echoed in the rough texture and unrodded folds of the shade beneath, its pulling mechanism, appropriately, being jute rope. It is also worth noting how well the shade fits below this beam, seeming to flow from it without interruption.

Light plays a dominant role in this kind of scheme, since it is the play of light that reveals the shadows and highlights of the surfaces. During the day, it pours in through the windows while at night discreet spotlights in the ceiling perform a diffusing function. Since lighting creates mood and atmosphere, it is well worth ensuring that you choose well, particularly in a kitchen where some kind of dual-purpose lighting is required–bright light for the work areas, and a more subtle, diffused light for the parts of the room where you eat and relax.

A collection of old wooden chairs picks up the texture and antique feel of the wood beams, their different outlines making a contrast of texture and shape with the paler colors and simple lines of the cupboards and table. Rough cream burlap chair cushions have been tied in position with natural rope–an echo of the texture which has been used for the shade mechanism.

In a scheme like this, even the kitchen utensils have been carefully considered, and are in the neutrals theme. Although this might seem purist, small splashes of bright or disparate colors would distract the eye and spoil the impression that this room makes. One of the advantages of opting for this sort of neutrals scheme in a kitchen is that it focuses interest on the activities that take place within the room, and the people that use it. Since kitchens are, in many houses, the heart of the home, this is a particularly successful concept for decorating because it gives the kitchen something of the intimate feel of a Vermeer painting. Color, if required, could be provided in the form of a large bulletin board for children's drawings and for favorite postcards, as well as the more mundane paperwork that invariably accompanies family life.

OPPOSITE *This small, antique pie safe has been painted cream, and the door frame decorated with a design of different vegetables, in natural colors. Although this has been hand-painted, a similar design could easily be created with stencils.*

A neutrals color theme works well for kitchens, particularly where, as here, natural wood has been used for almost all the surfaces, creating a rich interplay of texture and soft, pale color. The cream-colored range fits seamlessly into the overall scheme, its old-fashioned curved lines in keeping with the wooden beams, and further echoed by the different shapes of the kitchen chairs. Textural contrast is provided by the natural burlap shade, the chair cushions, and their rope ties. No strong color intrudes on this scheme.

Subtle shifts of pale tone are the
keynotes of this elegant Swedish-
style dining room. Simple lines
and a monochrome color scheme
play an important part in the
calm atmosphere, creating a
wonderful feeling of space and
light. Note how the detailing
around the cornices in a deeper
grayish-white helps to define the
shape of the room and draws
attention to the architecture. The
Gustavian look is one of purity
of line, restrained elegance, light,
simple, cool colors, and a
balanced arrangement of the
furniture. This room has been
kept simple, but sometimes the
look is highly decorated.

A Swedish-Style Dining Room

Loosely based on what is known as the Gustavian style, this dining room is elegant yet simple. It relies on the natural beauty of wood, delicately washed in pastel tones, so can be translated successfully to both town and country houses. At first glance, the room appears to be monochromatic and simple, with a minimal color scheme based on tones of off-whites and grays. However, a closer look reveals the elegance of the decoration and the wealth of delicate details, making this a sophisticated and serene scheme for a country dining room. It has been designed around the elegant Swedish dining table and chairs, which are painted in a pale dove gray. The detailing in the room is rich in different textures and patterns, and a range of neutral colors has been used for the curtains and chair covers, the painted furniture, the collections of glass and pewter, the table linen, and the china.

The original Scandinavian Gustavian style derives from the period of King Gustav III of Sweden in the eighteenth century, its hallmark being a purity of line, softened by the addition of pearly-gray, blue, cream, or white paint. It is the determination to paint every item of furniture that typifies the Scandinavian look, as much as the colors used, in particular the painting of the simple softwood boarded floors, which also helps to create the "clean" style. Much of the paint used in Scandinavia contains lime. This was the original preservative used in paint both in Northern Europe and elsewhere before modern chemicals took its place. The lime adds both a chalkiness and a luminosity to the finished effect and it is this subtle combination of opacity with sheen, often allowing some of the natural wood finish beneath to show through, that creates the final look.

Precisely because it is subtle and pale, you have to be extremely careful how you deal with the rest of the color palette in the room. In Scandinavian schemes, a particular soft palette of blue, gray, ocher, Indian red (red oxide), and occasionally yellow and a soft viridian is used. The key is to ensure that no single color dominates or stands out too sharply against the others, otherwise the look is lost.

This color palette is used in Scandinavian rooms, which receive cold north light, because the pale colors increase the amount of light in the room–a very important consideration in a climate where the winter days are extremely short. Painting over the wood introduces yet more light-reflective surfaces into the room and also helps to make relatively cheap softwoods look much smarter. In addition, the white paint picks up color from the underlying wood, a process which is often helped along by adding a little washed-down ocher and Indian red to the paint. The shade of blue used is important–it must contain enough yellow to be warm, without so much that it moves toward the greener end of the blue spectrum.

OPPOSITE *Pewter has a rich and wonderfully lustrous appearance. Its soft gray sheen blends well with many different color combinations but is shown off to great advantage against this distressed painted shelf. The solid, simple shapes combined with the reflectivity of the metal work particularly well in a restrained neutrals scheme.*

Painting the floorboards

There are various ways of creating pale-colored wood floors. Much depends on the surface that exists already. You can, if you wish, lime an ordinary wood floor using liming wax or paste, which will very effectively remove the "orange" look of a pine floor, for example. For this floor, which was already stained a fairly dark color, and had a paler center where a carpet had once been, a simple colorwash painted look was applied, which kept this change of tone intact.

you will need Sandpaper • Clear matt acrylic varnish • White pigment • Straightedge • Masking tape • Dove gray paint

1 Clean and lightly sand down the existing surface of the floor to remove any grease and to provide a key for the paint.

2 Using a mixture of acrylic varnish and white pigment, which has been well diluted with water, brush this onto the floor in one or two coats to soften the stained areas and make them look paler.

3 Use a straightedge to draw the lines for the double border on the floor. Using these marks as a guide, run three lines of masking tape, about 1 in (2.5 cm) apart from each other, a little way in from the baseboards all around the room.

4 Carefully paint between the lines of masking tape with a small roller or brush, using a pale dove gray paint. Leave to dry, then apply a thin coat of varnish to seal the paintwork.

Curtains with border

Simplicity is the keynote of these elegant curtains bordered with the same woven jacquard fabric in a contrasting color. Make lined curtains in the usual way, and follow the instructions here to add a border down the leading edges and along the lower edges prior to attaching the lining. The complete border is assembled, and the corner at the lower edge where the two pieces meet is mitered, before the border is joined to the curtain. The instructions are for one curtain.

you will need Curtain fabric and lining • Contrasting fabric for border • Sewing thread

1 For each curtain, cut one 8 in (20 cm) wide strip to the width of the curtain plus 4⅝ in (11.5 cm), and one 8 in (20 cm) wide strip to the length of the curtain plus 4⅝ in (11.5 cm). Fold the strips in half lengthwise, wrong sides together, and press. Now fold one end of the side border strip diagonally so that the end is even with the pressed fold; press and cut along this diagonal fold. Unfold the strip: you should have an outward-pointing V-shape. Do this to one end of the lower border strip as well.

2 With the strips unfolded and placed with their right sides together, join the pointed end of the side border to the pointed end of the lower border, taking a ⅝ in (1.5 cm) seam allowance, and stopping the stitching at each side ⅝ in (1.5 cm) from the edge. Carefully trim the seam and corner with a pair of sharp scissors, then turn the border right side out. Press the seam open.

3 With right sides together and raw edges even, position the border on the curtain. Clip into the seam allowance of the border at the mitered corner so it lies flat. Pin and stitch, with a ⅝ in (1.5 cm) seam allowance. Stitch into the mitered corner (rather than beginning the stitching there). Press the extra fabric of the border out of the way.

4 Press the border away from the main curtain. Now line the curtains in the usual way, making sure that the lining covers the raw edges of the seam that joins the curtain to the border.

Taking pride of place in the center of the dining table is a Wedgwood creamware tureen. Originally designed as functional china for use by the servants, its elegant simplicity has turned it into a valuable collector's item. It symbolizes the purity of color, line, and texture that is at the heart of any neutrals scheme.

Introducing light and texture

OPPOSITE BOTTOM *An antique chest has been painted and distressed in a shade of dark grayish-green, with the cream paint picking out the detailing. The silvery-gray pewter plates and the grayish-green foliage and cream flowers in a tall glass vase unify the color scheme.*

The paints used in this room have been carefully chosen from a range of historic paints to bring as much light into the room as possible, yet they are all earthy, soft shades of white instead of harsh, brilliant white. Instead of painting the room in one or two colors, four shades of off-white have been used to create interest and atmosphere. Lime white, which is the same shade as soft white limewash or distemper, covers the walls. Old white is used for the ceiling; off-white for the glazing bars on the windows; and a neutral, grayish-white on the baseboards and the door and window frames. These four paint shades work well together, add depth and focus to the color scheme, and create a subtle effect simply because they are all based on white, rather than being white tinted with a slight color.

The floor is also painted to continue the Swedish theme, and step-by-step instructions on how this is done are given on pages 72–73. There are many different methods for painting floors, and just as many different effects that can be achieved. However, in a Gustavian scheme, the aim is not to create a solid, opaque layer of color but to consider the floor as part of the entire scheme. In this room, some of the floor was originally black and so needed a careful treatment that would allow the dark stain to show through without being the most dominant feature.

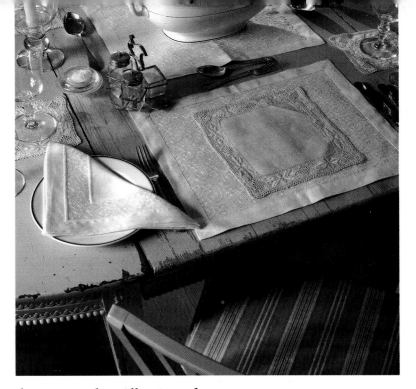

The sheen, life, and character provided by the bleached floor, coupled with the sunlight flooding in from the window, are what give this room its vitality. It cannot be over-emphasized how important this quality is in interior decorating, no matter how well you mix and match the colors, because without it a room will appear to be flat and uninteresting.

A muted, grayish-green has been added as a subtle accent color in the room to give the neutral tones something to bounce off. The leading edges of the curtains have heath green borders, and this green also appears in the thin stripe of the chair covers, the gingham lampshade in the corner, the collection of glasses arranged in the window, and the plants and greenery outside.

It is not just color that provides atmosphere, but color coupled with texture and the way the light plays on, reflects, and absorbs color. As discussed on pages 56–58, texture is not a fixed item—we perceive it only through light and the interplay of light with it, and in decorating this is a key element in choosing and combining colors.

As with all neutrals schemes, texture plays an important part in the success of this room's decoration. There are several clever uses of it, including the wide variety of linen on the table. The delicate white cotton placemats and small lace mats for the glasses add a splash of white to the table; beige linen mats pick out the taupe color of the chair covers and are carefully arranged to create intriguing layers of different textures on the table top. The carving on the side of the table and the lovely quality of peeling paint also add to this. The silver on the dining table and the collection of antique pewter plates bring a metallic quality to the scheme as well as extending the gray tones of the painted furniture. Antique, classic Wedgwood creamware adds the sophisticated texture of smooth, reflective porcelain and picks up the warm, creamy color of the curtains. The collection of glass plates on the large window introduces pattern, the line of antique wine glasses on the smaller window contains splashes of the heath green seen elsewhere in the dining room, and both add a translucent texture that brings a further luminous quality into the decorative scheme.

ABOVE *This table setting shows a subtle variety of pale tones and layers of different textures—from the painted distressed wood of the table, through the delicate worked threads of the white and cream embroidered table linen, to the smoothness of the silver and glassware.*

LEFT *With their deep shadows and brilliant highlights, the papery pure white flowers of these hydrangeas in a simple cream bowl demonstrate how pale colors reflect and absorb light. Even white is never all one tone—it changes with the quality of light.*

RIGHT *A collection of clear and green antique wine glasses, in a variety of shapes, stands on a windowsill where the light will catch it, and show the translucency of the glass off to perfection. In a similar way, a collection of glass ice plates has been arranged on another windowsill (see page 76).*

Fabric

To keep the typically Swedish quality of restrained elegance and concentrate the scheme on color and texture rather than pattern, a lightweight woven jacquard which is the color of unbleached cotton has been chosen for the curtains. The fabric has the textural quality of damask, which gives elegance to the room, and its creamy color creates a warm effect. The curtains hang from an ordinary rod. Edged with a wide heath green strip of the same fabric around the leading edges and along the hem (see pages 74–75 for instructions on how to do this), they have been allowed to pool slightly on the floor. There is no room here for a cornice or valance or even any fancy heading but a decorative feature has been made of the window by arranging a collection of antique glass plates on one window and green glass on another. The chairs have been covered in a woven ticking with narrow stripes of taupe, white, and heath green.

CHAPTER 3

yellows

The color of sunshine, yellow is one of the most uplifting and versatile colors to use in decoration. Ranging as it does from the palest of lemons, warm sunny cowslip, bright mustard, and egg yolk to rich, earthy ochers, golds, and other exotic Eastern shades, yellow contains a vast range of shades. It can be the color of the pale primroses of spring; of abundant summer flowers such as irises, roses, lilies, and sunflowers; of fields of wheat and corn in high summer–associations which have made the color a big success for Laura Ashley. It can be the rich, uninhibited, butter and mustard yellows of Provence and the Mediterranean; the elegant golds of royal palaces; or the spicy yellows of saffron and turmeric.

Yellow is a wonderful color for decoration. For a cold house that gets little sunshine, yellow can exact a transformation. Even adding a little yellow to a cold house painted in a harsh white can turn it into something much more welcoming. For those who want a bolder statement, rich, sunny yellows can be used as paint or paper on the walls, to give the effect of drenching the room in sunshine.

Yellow, being such a naturally bright color, has the capacity to startle and surprise, and it is worth exploiting its slightly eccentric quality. However, it can be difficult to find the right shade for a particular room. The yellow you first choose might be too sharp, too acid, too cold, or too orange, so it is worth testing out as large an area of the color as you can find before committing yourself. Nevertheless, once you have found the exact shade, you will no doubt be delighted with it. You can also mix yellow with other colors–cowslip combined with sapphire is an extremely successful combination for Laura Ashley. Increase the impact by introducing bold color combinations such as bright, china blue or scarlet, which, when used with a similarly saturated egg yolk yellow, make a warm, very vibrant scheme; or use soft blues, whites, or grays for a pale scheme.

Since yellow is one of the colors of sunshine, it is important to consider its contribution to the overall scheme. The existing color of any scheme can be subtly and sometimes even substantially altered by the color and tone of the light that falls on it, whether artificial or real. This means that not only can you compensate for a hard, cold, naturally blue light by using naturally warm yellow tones in the paintwork and fabrics, but so too can you use yellow-toned light.

Historical associations

Yellow was not used very much by interior decorators in the past, although it was favored by artists such as Van Gogh, Monet, and England's Bloomsbury Group, who liked its surprising and dashing qualities. It was also associated with royalty–Oriental emperors liked Chinese yellow, and a deeper shade was the favorite color of France's

Louis XIV, known as the Sun King. Yellow's association with gold has always made it seem both rich and exotic. Until the 1820s, when the more acidic, greenish, chrome yellow was first manufactured cheaply, most of the yellows used relied on the earth pigments of yellow ocher and raw sienna that occur naturally around the world.

One of the bravest uses of yellow was in Sir John Soane's drawing room at his house in Lincoln's Inn Fields, London, which relies on an almost unrelieved use of brilliant chrome yellow for both paintwork and fabrics. Unusually, the contrast to the yellow is a deep crimson, used to edge the silk curtains and to braid the upholstery. This is clever because the choice of red warms the acidity of the yellow and gives it more vibrancy.

More modern enthusiasts of decorating with yellow have been painters like Monet at his house in Giverny, France, and Duncan Grant and Vanessa Bell at Charleston in East Sussex, England. Monet's famous all-yellow dining room at Giverny uses a mid, bright blue as a contrast for the fabric and ceramics. Yellow was used at Charleston, and one of Duncan Grant's own designs from the 1930s, the primrose yellow and pale gray Grapes fabric (reintroduced by Laura Ashley in 1987), hangs in the garden room. A warmer yellow has also been used, with great panache, as the background color to the country house style of decorating in the second half of the twentieth century, using several shades of the same hue to create an unparalleled feeling of life. Yellow was popular in the 1950s and 1960s too, when primary colors were so fashionable.

The drawing room at Sir John Soane's early nineteenth century house in London is a perfect example of a bold use of yellow. A wonderfully bold chrome yellow has been used for both the walls and the magnificent silk curtains, which are bordered in deep crimson. The yellow is a brilliant contrast for the dark wooden furniture. Even the polished wooden floor has a strong yellowish tinge, no doubt reflecting yellow from the rest of the room.

Lemon yellow

The sharp, light, slightly acidic tones of lemon yellow can look marvelous in big, sunny modern rooms, accompanied by natural fabrics such as cottons or rustic, woven cloths. It is equally beautiful in silk, for an elegant, formal look. Lemon yellow can be combined successfully with a sharp lime green and white, or contrasted with a deep, warm blue which neutralizes the acidity and gives the whole scheme a softer, more gentle appearance. In a scheme where florals are used, it can be combined with other light colors, such as blues, greens, and apricots, to create a modern country house look using bleached wood furniture, perhaps, and stripped floors. Historically, lemon yellow was widely used to decorate French interiors during the Empire period. In very recent times, it has been combined, in a slightly warmer, more primrose-like tone, with pale gray which, like the blue, tends to remove the acidity but, unlike the blue, leaves a much cooler-looking scheme. It is also used as an ice-cream sorbet color, often combined with pistachio green and hot pink.

Butter yellow

The warmer, buttery yellows–colors often called cowslip, straw, buttercup, or sunflower yellow–are very versatile and easy to live with. They are ideal colors for country prints and create a wonderful sense of relaxation because they can evoke the soft, gentle sunshine of a spring day or, in more vibrant shades, the warmth of Provence. These yellows tend to enhance almost any space–whether it is a kitchen, bathroom, living room, or bedroom–because they can be paired with a whole range of other colors. They are particularly effective for wall colors, and combine well with a wide range of colors, such as clear blues, deep burgundy reds, and mid-toned greens, and are given crispness when combined with white.

Yellow ocher

Surprisingly, this dull, earthy yellow is also a versatile decorating color. It has a similar color palette to butter yellows, and was influenced by the colors of the East–saffron, turmeric, mustard, and ocher. Its dullness provides an excellent contrast for brighter hues such as turquoise, Indian red, electric blue and even some shades of pink. Yellow ocher is particularly valuable for achieving antiqued or distressed effects in paintwork. It frequently appears in Persian tile patterns, when it is often combined with cobalt blue and Indian red. It is also used in Europe, where the color occurs naturally in the earth in the form of ocher and sienna pigments.

Gold

This is one of the most popular accent colors to be used in the decorative arts because it enhances all sorts of room schemes, whether in the form of simple gilding on mirrors and

The sharply curving outlines of the fine antique creamware contrast with the softly billowing shapes of the orange and gold parrot tulips. The decorated plates in the background link both the color and the form of the flowers and china.

picture frames, on edgings and moldings, items made from brass, or in the gold lacquered furniture of the Louis XIV period. Gold, and muted old gold, can also be used in fabrics, such as those made by Fortuny, Genoese velvets, and Venetian damasks. Gold adds an unmistakable touch of luxury and elegance to any room, but has to be handled with great care to ensure that it looks distinguished. When combined with deep, rich colors such as red, purple, deep green, and deep blue, gold has a very regal appearance, reminiscent of exotic Eastern palaces.

Orange-yellow

This color ranges from the palest pastel apricot, through warm and rich marmalade-yellow to bright, primary orange. These shades can either be subtle, pale, and soft, adding just a hint of warmth to a white base, or they can be strident, strong colors that demand attention. The soft apricot shades are very easy to work with and blend well with blues, greens, and grays, making an excellent background to the patina and depth of color of any of the woods with reddish tones.

Texture

Texture is important in yellow color schemes because the interplay of light and dark on shades of yellow can give dramatic effects. It is a very responsive color for paint effects–flat finishes can be used or broken paint effects, such as colorwashing, sponging, or stippling over other colors. Applied as a transparent glaze, either in acrylics or oil paints, over a white ground (or indeed over existing white-painted walls), the effect will be light, bright, and fresh. Applied over a darker tone–such as deeper shades of beige or light brown–the effect will be deep and warm, bringing to life the background color (a technique that is often seen in Tuscany). This look works well when much paler neutrals are chosen for the fabrics, with the odd spot of brighter, richer color–terra-cottas and mid-blues, perhaps–acting as a contrast. Brilliant yellows can also be used with more sober colors, to pick out details–door and window frames, chair and picture rails, and crown moldings. Walls can be divided to allow the lower part to be painted plain bright yellow, while the upper part, above a chair rail, is papered in yellow and white checks or candy stripes, for example.

When bright and sunny, yellow translates best to surfaces which are reflective. It works well for walls, but has to be used with more care for furniture, although pieces painted in antiqued yellow ocher can look very

Yellow can be warm or cool. In this room, the walls have been colorwashed in ocher, and the curtains have an apricot design on a yellow background.

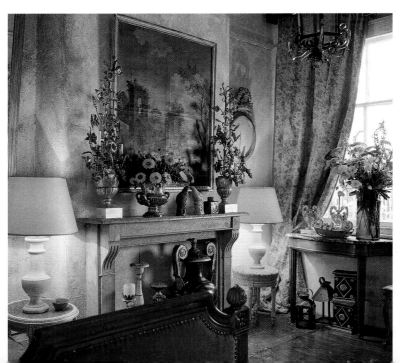

successful, particularly if their borders are picked out in deep red or olive green. With the use of gold, all sorts of shiny and silky textures are possible, and rich gold braids, gilt-framed mirrors and paintings, and gilded furniture all add a touch of glamour and ornamentation to a room. Gold and gilt finishes need to be handled with care because they can sometimes be overpowering and fussy. They tend to look best when used sparingly, or in surprising places. One large, gilded item in what is otherwise a fairly plain room can look striking and stylish, particularly when contrasted with plain fabrics, simple furniture and pale, waxed wood.

A cool citrus yellow has been used for these walls. The sofa fabric contains no yellow, and is patterned in green and terra-cotta. Avoiding repeating colors too slavishly, but picking ones that harmonize instead, creates a relaxed, lived-in feel to the room.

For a rich, opulent look, choose silks, damasks, brocades, and velvets in the more golden shades of yellow; for fresh, summery appeal, choose yellow cottons in reps, sailcloths, and cambrics. Yellow is one of the more popular colors in Far Eastern textile design, and is often a background color in saris, for example, so it is worth looking in ethnic shops for bright yellow silks.

Furniture and decorative objects can also introduce a textured yellow theme to a room. Rattan furniture, straw baskets and hats, glazed yellow ceramic tiles, and terra-cotta urns with their rims dipped in yellow glaze are all ideal.

Fabrics

Yellow is a particularly suitable color for fabric, especially as a background color for other patterns or an accent color for floral designs. Along with pink, yellow is one of the most popular color motifs in floral patterns of all descriptions. An extensive range of yellow-based patterns is available, from small sprigged country motifs to big blowzy cabbage rose designs, most of them combined with green and blue. Provençal cotton uses wonderful deep, rich yellows, in floral and geometric patterns, mixed with bright blues and deep reds, for a sophisticated patterned effect. Often these brilliantly printed fabrics do not contain any white, and it is this depth of strong color, combined with yellow, that gives them their characteristic intensity and charm.

English country house florals are available in a marvelously varied range of patterns, often with birds, insects, and flowers. They frequently contain dull shades of gold and yellow, combined with mid-greens, blues, and pinks. They can look particularly effective when the colors are subdued and appear to have been faded by the sun, or years of use.

When choosing a suitable fabric, much depends on the depth of color in the yellow itself. For the gold end of the spectrum, you have the opportunity to plump for damasks,

OPPOSITE *Cowslip yellow combines particularly well with chambray blue in this drawing room, which shows a variety of yellow floral chintzes. White, used here for the colorwashed boards, helps to lift the overall color scheme and give it a lighter feel, in an interesting twist to the normal decorating idiom where the boards are generally dark and the furniture pale. The patchwork quilt on the wall provides a decorative and unusual backdrop.*

dobbies, brocades, rich silks, and opulent crushed velvets, which are used mainly for their reflective and luminous qualities. If you move toward the more lemony yellows, then simple, natural fabrics–linens and cottons–are ideal because they enhance the fresh attributes of these shades, as do silks and chintzes. On the whole, the more acid yellows, which contain plenty of green, lend themselves to clean, crisp fabrics–sharp cottons, for example, or glazed chintzes. Yellow and white make a good clear mixture in ginghams, candy-striped cottons, sailcloths, and canvases, and yellows, plums, and deep blues mix well in rich floral patterns where white is excluded. Yellows and greens make fresh, light prints. Old gold and ruby red are used in many exotic, Far Eastern fabrics and patterns, while Turkish and Moorish designs combine saffron and cobalt blue.

Yellow provides a more interesting contrast for deep colors than white, and can be used in small ways to bring a color scheme based on these rich colors to life. Cushions, tie-backs, braiding, and piping in bright, buttery yellows work particularly well with deep blues and greens. You can contrast these colors with Victorian crimson for a strong scheme, in richly woven and highly patterned fabrics. For an Italian Renaissance look, consider mixing yellow with terra-cotta on figured grounds, such as damask or brocade. Gold braid and tassels can transform relatively simple curtains and drapes into something much grander, as can gilding a curtain pole (see pages 186–187), the edges of a piece of painted furniture, a lampstand, or a photo frame.

Yellow decorative details

Yellow is one of the strongest colors in nature's repertoire, much used by plants for attracting insects for the purpose of pollination. Yellow flowers can sing out in any room, from great armfuls of spring flowers, such as daffodils or tulips, to the wonderfully strong architectural shapes of sunflowers, so beloved of Van Gogh, whose love of yellow was second to none. As a change from flowers, bowls of yellow fruits can look stunning. You could mix lemons with limes for a sharp contrast, fill a low wooden bowl with honey-colored pears, or, in a contemporary room, use exotic yellow fruits such as star fruits and honey melons that have unusual shapes. Other details could include china, chosen to complement the style of the room. A country-style living room could show off a collection of plates with bright yellow borders and central floral patterns, while a yellow kitchen might be decorated with rustic yellow-glazed Mediterranean earthenware.

Walls and fabrics can be stamped or stenciled (see page 199)–try gold on white, on navy blue, or on crimson for a rich contrast. You could cover the whole of a wall with an antique patchwork quilt that is predominantly yellow, or display a collection of yellow paintings, perhaps with a common, linking theme.

This light, well-proportioned room in a converted barn has a wealth of interesting architectural features—exposed beams, a beautiful wood floor, and the bonus of attractive views through the windows. A simple decorating scheme such as this one, which uses flat expanses of plain color, helps to focus interest on the architectural features while keeping the sense of light and space.

A Yellow & White Living Room

A large, light room is a joy to decorate, provided you take account of the architectural features and create a scheme that enhances rather than working against them. This is a room in a converted barn at the coast, and it is decorated for the relaxed simplicity and casual lifestyle of a family weekend retreat. The windows look out to sea, and it is an ideal room for easy, summer living.

Yellow was chosen for its warmth, and white was added to create lightness. The colors are kept as solid blocks to enhance the modernity of the barn, and the only pattern used is in the woven ticking stripe for an armchair and the painted cushions and curtains. These were hand-painted in a deliberately simple, almost abstract, design to continue the contemporary feel of the room.

Using pale cowslip yellow and white, with touches of sky blues and sea greens, accentuates the light and airy atmosphere in this sunny, seaside room. The pale bleached wood of the polished floors and the roof timbers requires a simple decorative scheme that allows you to appreciate its natural beauty, texture, and tone rather than be distracted by other details. The overall effect is similar to the bleached appearance of driftwood, which is appropriate as this house is situated close to the ocean.

The choice of yellow for the walls has helped to add a touch of warmth, and the texture and consistency of the paint is also an important factor in this. A flat, dense paint that absorbs light will counteract any coldness, while looking and feeling warm. The yellow walls are an inspired choice: they offer the simplicity and straightforwardness of white or off-white, but cut down the glare that might otherwise be present in such a large room with so much glass.

Off-white has been chosen for the largest item of furniture in the room—the three-seater traditional sofa—and yellow has been used for the piping. This subtle and understated contrast works extremely well and is an idea that is well worth copying. The yellow piping provides the necessary outline without becoming too prominent, so it adds sculptural shape to the piece of furniture without distracting the eye from its overall form. Sea green and sky blue are both used as accent colors, seen in the paints used for the curtains and pillows, in their contrasting piping, and in the solid blocks of color formed by the two upright chairs and plain cushions.

Plain-colored, textured weaves and simple geometric stripes help to create the contemporary and very relaxed feel of this room. The cushions and the leading edges of the curtains have been hand-painted. Inexpensive muslin is an ideal fabric for painting, being both solid and dense enough to provide the equivalent of the artist's canvas. An alternative is the thick Indian cotton that is used here. You can use regular latex paint,

OPPOSITE *Here you can see the deep, egg yolk yellow piping on the sofa arms and box cushions. It makes an excellent, subtle but clear contrast with the slub weave of the off-white sofa fabric. The yellow theme is picked up in one of the painted pillows, with a pattern that incorporates blue and green as well, and a piped blue border. A plain green pillow makes a simple, strong counterfoil to the painted design.*

OPPOSITE *The far end of the same yellow room reveals an unexpectedly deep color—a rich, warm mid-blue—painted on a curved wall that continues the line of the hall. Although the room does not require this contrast, it is nevertheless a bonus and well worth copying in a similarly L-shaped room, or large alcove. Make sure that the contrasting color ties in, as this does, with the decoration of the whole room, otherwise the effect may be jarring. Solid blocks of contrasting color are working here with the positioning of the plain green chair against the blue wall and the solid yellow chair with two pillows, one in plain blue and one in plain green.*

RIGHT *Simple, well-constructed wood furniture fits very well with this decorative scheme which is equally simple. The modern, clean lines of the table reflect the style of the room's architecture. If you are unable to match your furniture to the color scheme in this way, you could paint the furniture—even inexpensive items can be made to marry with a scheme if painted in suitable colors.*

artist's acrylics, or fabric paints. If you keep to a simple motif and a repeating design, you do not need the talent of Picasso to create surprisingly good results. Instructions for painting the pillows are given on pages 96–97.

If you wish to experiment with the color scheme, it would be easy to take its principal features and reverse them, painting the walls green or blue, with a yellow alcove or recessed area (see opposite), using a yellow and white, or blue and white, striped fabric, and so on. A simple color palette of four colors, of which two are the principal performers and two the chorus or background, is a good basis for a decorative scheme. If the colors are even in tone, as they are here with the exception of the white, they will give a sense of uniformity and tranquility to the scheme. Tonal contrast will create a stronger, more dramatic impression.

Painting the pillows

Fabric can be painted in much the same way that any other surface is painted, but to prevent the paint from spreading and running you can size the fabric with a coat of diluted polyvinyl acrylic first. You can use fabric paints, acrylic paints, or regular latex paint, all of which are washable, provided you handwash the fabric with care and do not wring or tumble-dry it. Use any simple design that takes your fancy; stripes, wavy lines, circles, triangles, or spots. The paint does not have to adhere uniformly to the fabric—part of the charm of this design is its unevenness.

you will need Fabric (natural fibers and light colors are easiest) • Contrasting fabric, for piping • Piping cord • Sewing thread • Zipper, 2 in (5 cm) less than size of pillow • Polyvinyl acrylic (optional) • Fabric paints, acrylic paints, or latex paints • Pillow form • Sewing machine with zipper foot

1 Prepare the fabric by laying it on a board or waterproof surface, and stretch it taut, marking out with architect's tape the area for the painted design. Start to create the design using acrylic paints and a medium-sized artist's brush. It is most effective to work freehand, but if you are unsure of your painting skills you can practice on a spare piece of fabric first.

2 If you use more than one color, keep a separate brush for each color, and finish painting one colorway before adding the next. It is best to let the first color dry completely before applying the second if the panels of color will touch one another. This prevents the colors from bleeding into each other. If using fabric paints, fix them according to the manufacturer's directions.

3 Cut out the front and back of the pillow, leaving a ⅝ in (1.5 cm) seam allowance all around. Cut out 2 in (5 cm) wide strips of green fabric on the bias, and join together with diagonal seams until they fit the circumference of the pillow. Wrap the strips over the piping cord and machine baste next to the cord. Lay the piping along the seamline of the pillow front, with the cord facing inward. Stitch in place. Clip into the seam allowance of the piping at the corners so the piping will go around the corners smoothly.

4 Place open zipper, face down, on piping along bottom edge of pillow front and align the teeth with the stitching. Baste. Stitch through zipper tape and piping seam allowance, ⅛ in (3 mm) from the teeth. Turn under both seam allowances and close zipper so the folded edge meets the piping over the zipper. Baste, then stitch ¼ in (6 mm) from folded edge. Stitch across both ends of zipper up to piping. With right sides together and zipper open, stitch the pillow pieces together. Clip corners, turn right side out, and press.

This bedroom has been painted in four shades of yellow to create a subtle interplay of light and shade which emphasizes its quirky architecture. A collection of straw hats continues the yellow theme. Hints of greens, browns, aquas, soft blues, and ochers can be seen in the dust ruffle and quilt, and ocher yellow and smoky turquoise have been picked out for trimming the bedlinen. The decorative gilded lamp base and mirror add a further golden glow to the room.

A Yellow Bedroom

OPPOSITE *The eye is drawn to the interestingly sloped ceilings of this room by the careful choice of toning paint shades for the different planes of the wall and ceiling surfaces. This use of tone helps to emphasize the shadows and gives depth and structure to the whole room.*

BELOW *A close-up of the baseboard shows how three shades of yellow and white have been used for this area, including deep ocher for the baseboard. The yellow and white check pillow on the chair picks up the theme.*

This large, square bedroom has been given an almost uniformly yellow color scheme, but one with a difference–what might appear at first glance to be one yellow is actually several shades of one hue. The shades of yellow that have been chosen are particularly subtle and very warm, created from a soft earthy shade of yellow ocher blended with white, and together they create interest and add light and shade to the room. The simple color scheme is almost Shaker-like in its appeal, although it is warmed by the varied patterns of the antique quilt on the bed, the pretty floral linen of the dust ruffle, and the rich variety of textures, including old pine, wicker, straw, sisal, and the peeling, creamy paint on the head and foot of the bed. The scheme is kept light, fresh, and feminine with the sprigged white voile curtains and the yellow check shade.

Simplicity is the keynote of this scheme, and as a result the architectural interest of the room's sloping ceilings is emphasized. The effect is both warm and light, which is particularly useful in a bedroom such as this which has relatively small windows, and the yellow glows from the sunlight streaming in.

Four different shades of yellow were chosen from an historic paint range. Three separate shades of yellow were painted on the walls, a pale yellow on the baseboards, and cream on the ceiling. The four shades are an early nineteenth-century hay yellow which is bright but not excessively hot; a bright straw; a bright earthy cane color which originated in Italy; and the yellow used by the famous British designer John Fowler for the staircase at Sudbury Hall, Derbyshire, England. A different shade has been used for each wall to create a lovely tonal effect of the various yellows working together to give atmosphere and light. These slightly earthy, muted, dusty yellows combine beautifully with the old gold-colored linen in the room and look marvelous in old country houses.

If you are going to opt for a simple, painted scheme like this one, the quality and texture of the paint is extremely important because the way it reflects or absorbs light will affect the color and warmth of the whole room. Paint should be chosen with care. For this room, paints with the texture of distemper were used instead of acrylic. These flat paints look very effective on the surface of old plaster walls. Therefore, it pays to spend a little more time and money choosing not only the right color of paint, but the appropriate type for the job. Always do a small test on one corner of the wall first to check that you like both the color and the finish.

If you wanted to create a little more decoration in this kind of scheme, stamping a very subtle pattern on the walls, perhaps in a dusty toning blue or green, would be effective without altering the simple, country-style appeal, but beware of using too much pattern if you want to focus attention on the architectural detail.

Fabrics

A major feature of this room is the beautifully worked patchwork quilt. The paisley on top of the quilt features a mixture of yellows, beiges, browns, whites, and grays, which contrast with plains and stripes on the underside in a range of complementary colors. Sometimes old quilts were made from men's shirts as a practical way of using up discarded clothing. Some quilts were made from Victorian dress fabrics whose patterns have become a source of print design today. Quilts are wonderful heirlooms and a beautiful, antique quilt like this one can act as a starting point for a whole decorative scheme if you pick out a couple of key colors for the walls and curtains.

You can quite easily re-create these quilts today with a sewing machine, using a combination of stripes and checks. Many of these old quilts were plain on one side and patterned on the other, and were quilted using attractive scrolling patterns, some of which were traditional and had been passed down from generation to generation. These, too, can be worked using a sewing machine, and many informative books are available on the subject. When making up a quilt of this kind, decide whether to opt for toning or contrasting colors and then plan the design accordingly. Be careful not to combine bright and subtle colors, as the brights will stand out far too vividly and spoil the uniform appearance of the quilt.

The other fabrics in the room include the floral linen dust ruffle around the bed, which picks up the golds and creams in the rest of the room, and also appears as a pillow on the antique wooden chair. The cowslip check shade continues the yellow theme and the white voile curtains add light and a soft, fresh touch.

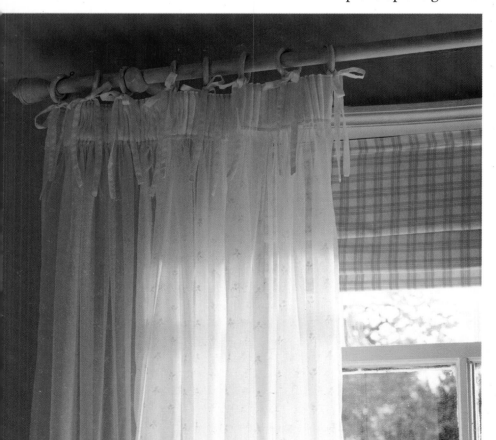

LEFT *Mixing two different kinds of fabrics at the windows adds textural interest to the decorative scheme. The sheer voile curtains have been hung from a yellow-painted pole with wooden rings, with small ties decorating the points where the curtains are fixed to the rings themselves. The voile is the decorative element, and the shade is the practical window covering—a reversal of the normal practice.*

RIGHT *A collection of straw hats emphasizes the textural elements in this room and makes an attractive contrast with the straw-colored surface of the walls. The hat-pegs are made of wood, which creates further texture in the room.*

Trimmed bedlinen

This simple technique can be used to add interest to plain white bedlinen. Contrasting, toning, or matching ribbon or tape can be applied along the edge of the top sheet, and all around the pillowslips, in a single or double row. Here, yellow and green ribbons and cotton tape were used, to pick up the colors in the room. Make sure the ribbon and tape are colorfast, and are compatible in washing terms with the bedlinen. Preshrink the ribbon or tape if it is not already preshrunk.

you will need

For trimming pillowslips
For each pillowslip: ⅝ in (1.5 cm) wide green cotton tape • ⅝ in (1.5 cm) wide yellow cotton tape • Matching sewing threads
For trimming sheets
For each sheet: 1¼ in (3 cm) wide green-and-yellow ribbon • 1⅜ in (3.5 cm) wide yellow ribbon • Matching sewing threads

Pillowslips

1 Lightly mark a line about 2 in (5 cm) from all four edges of the pillowslip and pin the tape along this line. For flanged pillows, pin the tape along the inner edge of the flange. Stitch along the inner edge of the tape. To miter each corner, fold the tape back on itself and stitch diagonally between the inner and outer corners. Trim along the diagonal seamline, leaving a narrow seam allowance. Fold the tape at right angles to the previous position and pin and stitch down the next edge. Repeat for the other three edges.

2 Take the green tape and tuck it under the outer edge of the yellow tape, again mitering the corners; pin and then stitch through both the yellow and the green tapes, using the yellow thread. Now pin and stitch the outer edge of the green tape, using the green thread. Neatly tie off the ends of the threads and trim, making sure there are no loose ends.

Sheet

1 Press a fold along the length of the yellow ribbon so that one side is slightly wider than the other. Wrap the folded ribbon over the edge of the sheet, with the wider side at the back. Stitch in place, being careful to keep the fold of the ribbon in contact with the edge of the sheet, and ensuring that the stitching goes through the sheet and both layers of the ribbon. Keep the ribbon and sheet taut as you stitch, to prevent puckering. Turn under the ends of the ribbon to finish.

2 Using a pencil and ruler, mark a line about 2½ in (6.5 cm) away from the binding. Pin and stitch one edge of the yellow-and-green ribbon along this line, turning under both the ends. Now stitch the other edge of the ribbon, working in the same direction as before to keep the ribbon smooth and prevent it puckering. Neatly tie off the ends of the threads and trim, making sure there are no loose ends.

YELLOWS

BELOW *Another texture is added in the collection of old wicker suitcases which echo the paint colors. When looking for special decorative elements to create atmosphere in a room, you do not have to be too precise or formal. A collection of cases, hatboxes, or baskets piled in a corner, on top of a dresser, or hanging from simple wooden poles or pegs, looks wonderful in a country-style setting such as this.*

BELOW RIGHT *Several patterns have been mixed in this room. The quilt contains a variety of patterns, with its mixture of florals, paisley, and stripes. The dust ruffle of the bed is in a pretty, traditional floral pattern in linen, in the same soft yellow as the walls. Mixing pattern in this way works well provided you ensure that cohesive elements link the schemes—for example, you could match the size of the patterns, the colors they include, or the style of pattern.*

LEFT *The attractive wooden furniture in this room is old pine, with some wicker and rush, which echoes the country style. This pretty rush-seated chair goes very well with the warm yellow walls and looks completely at home in the room. The sheer voile curtains add a white, translucent quality against the solid, plain, painted walls.*

RIGHT *The introduction of bright orange in the lampshade and the flower arrangement helps to lift the color scheme in this bedroom. The gilding on the mirror and lamp base picks up the yellow theme but in a different texture–this time in a more elegant way–and the brilliant glossy green of the foliage in the arrangement provides a striking contrast to the orange chrysanthemums.*

CHAPTER 4

greens

Green is one of the most versatile colors in decoration, just as it provides a background role in nature–you only need to look in a garden to see how many colors green harmonizes with. Its popularity is increasing in the 1990s because it is associated with the outdoors and is therefore in tune with the growing interest in environmental issues. Tranquil, relaxing, and peaceful, green is, in its own way, one of the more neutral decorating colors, and as a consequence it can be mixed successfully with many others, tending to take on their character in the process.

Green is made principally from blue and yellow, so its character also varies according to how much of these two colors is used in its composition. The "balance color," it is located halfway between the warm and cool colors on the color wheel. Nature shows us the almost unlimited range of greens that are available, from the sappy greens of fresh grass shoots, new buds, unfurling leaves and young seedlings to the richer, darker greens of rose leaves, oak leaves, conifers, and many other trees and plants. Perhaps as a result of green's connection with nature, it is considered a cooling, restful color.

Paints and papers

Very dark greens, which are often called forest or bottle greens, can make good background colors for rooms in which the chief color accent is a strong contrast, and can be used for painted walls or as the background color in a dark patterned paper, for example. They provide a good foil for antique wooden furniture–particularly old pine–to create a strong, solid look.

Dark greens, such as forest, hunting, bottle, olive, and racing greens, were much used in Victorian and Edwardian decorative schemes in both the United States and Britain, and were especially popular color choices for hallways and studies. They were also used for painted kitchen furniture of the same period, and a particular shade of dark bluish-green, known as Paris green, has become the brand color of Laura Ashley. This shade is popular for paintwork in European countries such as France and Italy; particularly on the outsides of white houses; and for garden furniture.

For external paintwork, dark green gloss or flat oil paint is associated with the Art Nouveau movement, when it was often combined with purple in various intricately worked designs. The very dark bluish-green of the Paris Métro signs and railings is a typical example of this. A similar dark green was often used for painting front doors and, occasionally, whole houses, especially the clapboard houses popular in Scandinavia and parts of the United States. It is also frequently used for outdoor garden furniture, such as ironwork benches or metal, collapsible, garden seats. Painting new fences or structures such as wooden trellises or obelisks in dark green helps them to blend into the

OPPOSITE *So predominant in nature, green, more than any other color, links the house with the garden. In this boot room in a country house, green provides an appropriate color scheme in a range of shades and tones, from the brilliant emerald green of the painted outhouse door to the hunting greens of the gardening boots and coats, while the vegetable print on the curtains continues the garden theme.*

background of a garden and merge with the surrounding foliage. Green is also an obvious choice for a garden room, because it continues the verdant theme created by the plants themselves.

William Morris used green a great deal in his Arts and Crafts designs, although the shades varied considerably from rich bottle greens to pale, leafy greens. Multicolored chinoiserie, floral, sprigged, and other informal wallpaper patterns all feature green as a coordinating color, and this is often picked out for the furnishings in the rest of the room. Green is also used in many Laura Ashley wallpapers, either in its own right or as a background or secondary color.

Fabrics

Certain themes and styles have particular associations with green. It has always formed a major color theme in many chintz patterns, usually as the background to another color. Many of the Arts and Crafts textiles used a deep shade of green for the background color, particularly the birds and beasts patterns made popular by William Morris at the turn of the century. Crude greens were popular in the 1950s, sharp acid green and white striped cotton was especially fashionable in the 1970s, but in the 1990s greens have become softer and more suited to the increased interest in conservation.

Originally it was difficult to produce convincing greens in fabrics, and the color was not successfully manufactured as a fabric dye until the 1830s. Until then, green was created for chintzes by printing blue on yellow. The yellow dyes have faded faster than the blue ones, which is why antique floral chintzes today often have blue foliage.

Deep bottle green velvet is a perennial favorite, especially when used for curtains and upholstery, while chenille is enjoying a well-deserved revival in popularity. Both have a wonderfully rich, traditional feel, with overtones of gentlemen's clubs, the green baize of billiard tables, and dark green Victorian paintwork. In recent years, tartans, such as the well-known dark green and navy Black Watch pattern, have become increasingly popular, and different green-based tartans are often mixed together, employing one for a pillow cover, and another, perhaps, for the chair on which it sits.

This room demonstrates how well the Laura Ashley range of fabrics, in dark green, burgundy, and taupe, work together. It also shows how much of the decorator's job of choosing harmonizing colorways is done for you when you pick fabrics, papers, and paints from coordinated ranges. Mixing various patterns together, as here, gives an interestingly varied effect that looks natural and relaxed.

Glass and china

Wonderful, subtle shades of green are found in glassware, from the pale greenish tones of modern, inexpensive recycled glass and what is literally bottle green–the color of dark green bottles–to the more elegant deep greens of English and Venetian glassware popular in the nineteenth century. Dark green china is also available, from sturdy, simple French café-style cups and saucers in porcelain, to the cabbage leaf and vine leaf designs. Heavily textured and glazed in various shades of green, from deep olive to emerald, they look as if they are made from real leaves. Fine Regency china often had a border of sharp lettuce green on plain white ware, and this design is still used today. Green glazes are also very popular for rustic pottery and ironware.

Dark greens

Shades of dark green can vary quite considerably, depending on the quantities of blue, black, and yellow that are mixed to make the green. Equally, dark green is known by different names in different places. In the United States it has long been called Brunswick green, whereas it is usually known in Britain as forest or bottle green. Other very similar shades of dark green include hunting green, racing green, olive green, and

This brilliant combination of terra-cotta and green–colors that are diametrically opposite on the color wheel–makes a very strong statement in this room at the Sir John Soane Museum in London. The gold relieves and brightens the color contrast, as does the introduction of paler green, and pattern, in the carpet in the foreground.

Paris green. These are all classic colors which are historic in conception yet look neither dated nor dull. They translate so well to the country that they are very popular for traditional outdoor clothes, such as coats, jackets, and pants.

Olive green was particularly popular in the late nineteenth century, often as a background color to more brightly printed fabrics and papers. It can appear drab when used on its own, but looks effective when lifted with lighter colors, such as yellowish beiges and creamy whites. Bronze and gilt can also go particularly well with olive green, and furniture painted in this color can have its handles, borders, and edges picked out in gold. This is easily done using modern, cream-based gilt products.

Blue-greens

The range of blue-greens—which includes jade, teal, viridian, fir green, and emerald—is large, and at the point of turquoise it becomes hard to decide whether the color is fundamentally blue or green. It simply depends how much of each color is used in the composition. A greenish turquoise has become extremely popular in interior decoration for painting wood furniture, fixtures, and fittings.

Blue-green precious and semi-precious stones play a large part in the countries from which they originate. Eastern ceramics make extensive use of turquoise (the gemstone, turquoise, was first found in Turkey) and frequently combine it with russet red and a strong, cerulean blue as well as with ocher. Similar colorways are to be found in the prints of the Arts and Crafts movement, and occasionally in Art Deco designs. Jade is the sacred stone of the Orient (the translucent emerald green jade, known as "imperial," is the most precious form) and New Zealand greenstone has great significance for Maoris.

Gray-greens

These are a particularly soft shade of green, with a considerable amount of white added to a base color mixed from a bluish green. They include sage, moss, and misty green. Gray-green is an extremely restful color for decoration but tends to be used only rarely as a principal color in a scheme. It normally provides a secondary color for brighter, but equally soft, colors such as apricot or pale powder pink. It has been used extensively in printing fabric, and is a favorite choice for Swedish painted wood and furniture. A gray-green was also much used by the Shakers and it works extremely well for very plain, painted furniture, sometimes with a contrasting border color, such as terra-cotta or soft dusty pink.

Silver and glassware look particularly good set against a soft gray-green background, as does pewter, and a silver-greenish gray was often used as a glaze for Chinese porcelain made in the Sung dynasty (about 1000–1300 AD).

Light greens include pale moss green, apple green, aquamarine, mint, heath green, and pistachio. Other light greens are eau-de-nil, much used in the 1930s as a background color in interior decoration, and a more astringent, sharper, green, often combined with white. Eau-de-nil is often seen as the perfect complementary backdrop to antique furniture, particularly the brighter woods like mahogany or rosewood, and for antique paintings. It has provided the background for many English country house schemes, in which other similarly soft colors–powder blues, pale pinks, and lemony yellows–are combined in floral chintzes, tapestries, and faded antique Eastern carpets. Because it successfully absorbs the light, eau-de-nil is easy to live with and easy to combine with other colors, creating a neutral, passive, reflective mood.

Light greens

The fresh mossy greens are also used frequently in contemporary designs, in geometric prints such as stripes and checks, and sometimes combined in floral patterns with acid yellows and bright cobalt blues. Other light greens, such as apple green, mint, and pistachio, go well with other soft ice-cream colors. When dealing with these very bright colors, you need to think carefully about the paints, papers, and fabrics that you will be using and their degree of reflectivity. A flat finish is usually the most successful for this sort of color scheme, because a reflective, shiny paint, for example, could make the colors appear to be too dominant and intrusive.

Lime green and pea green belong in this category. There is a particular shade of bright yellow-green which is very strong and makes an extremely vivid statement, so you need to plan carefully before using it. Nevertheless, it is a marvelous accent color within a decorative scheme. It appeared in some Art Nouveau designs, was also used occasionally by England's Bloomsbury Group, and again appeared in some of the prints of the 1950s, often combined with earth colors such as orange and brown. It can look even fresher when used with other strong shades of blue, purple, or yellow, and appears very bright when combined with white or gold.

Bright yellow-greens

OPPOSITE *The billiard room at Wightwick Manor in England shows the prevailing influence of William Morris, the father of the Arts and Crafts movement. His influence extends throughout the whole house. This photograph illustrates the use of toning colors–here, a deep blue and soft sage green–which were such a trademark of the prints designed by William Morris. Stylized shapes of natural forms, such as birds, beasts, and flowers, were the principal feature of most of the Arts and Crafts textiles and wallpaper designs, many of which are in production again today.*

Fresh and cheerful, light green is one of the easiest colors to live with, as this living room in pale moss green demonstrates. It is one of the best colors to use as a foil for the rich tones of mahogany and other fine woods. To give it life and depth, a variety of different shades of green have been incorporated in the upholstery, which gives the color scheme harmony without appearing dull. Touches of blue and pink give vitality to this traditional country house decorative scheme.

A Green Living Room

OPPOSITE *Plain, painted walls in pale moss green, with a deeper green crown molding, provide a delicate foil for the distressed gold frame of the oil painting above the fireplace, which has been painted in the same shade of green. A plain background such as this plays an important part in unifying a color scheme that employs mixed color and pattern, and makes a link with the tonal striped wallpaper on the other walls.*

This large and spacious room has some unusual architectural features, notably the exposed stonework between the windows, the deep window recesses, the paneled walls on one side of the room, and the relatively low ceiling. To counteract the effect of the latter, a light-colored and fresh-looking decorating scheme was needed, which also increased the amount of light in the room.

The room forms part of a large country house, built several centuries ago, in a monastic settlement in the East of England. It is important, when planning any kind of decorative scheme, to try to keep the flavor of the period in which the house was built, and also to consider its architecture. This green and white living room is a case in point. The ceilings of the room are very low for its large proportions, so a light and sunny scheme is appropriate to enhance the space. The simple, chintzy look, with its predominantly light green theme, is particularly suitable for the room's country setting. The paneled walls are painted to match the tonal striped wallpaper in pale moss. The windows all face onto views of grass and trees, and the interior green theme picks up this metaphor and translates it into a suitably "gardenesque" idiom. Green is ideal for country house interiors because it combines well not only with the view through the windows but with any arrangements you make of garden flowers or foliage. Some of the most exquisite arrangements are composed entirely from foliage, and these simple green, or sometimes green and white, arrangements, loosely arranged in a large ceramic bowl or jug, are ideal for this kind of setting.

The room has been decorated in classic country house style, using soft greens which will fade beautifully in the sun over the years. It is a room ideally suited for summer, with a door that opens straight into the yard. Pale moss, which is very similar to the color of the lawn, has been chosen as the main wall color to link the room with the outdoors. An interesting mixture of large-scale floral prints has been used for the curtains and pillows to give the impression that pretty yellow, blue, and pale pink cottage garden flowers are growing through green shrubbery. The antique and distressed gilded picture frames add warmth and faded elegance to the room.

Mixing patterns and colors

It is very easy, when using pattern, to become ruled by it and use too much of the same pattern throughout, which looks extremely contrived and is ultimately unrestful. You need to mix the patterns while keeping to a common theme, such as similar colors or textures. The patterns used in this room are quite varied and, as you can see, various tones and shades of the principal color, green, have been used. You will find that if you opt for this kind of mixed pattern effect, you do not need to be too concerned about achieving an exact color match. You can use various shades of green–some with more yellow and some with more blue–to produce a varied effect, but you need to make sure they have roughly the same tonal value.

In this drawing room, different shades of green in similar tones have been used and blue has been introduced as a secondary color. This makes the scheme more lively and less contrived. Some people will try to tell you that blue and green do not go together, but these colors can be used extremely successfully provided you keep the proportions in balance. Combined as they are here with white, they create an overall feeling of freshness and coolness, while spicing the mixture. It also helps if you keep the fabrics similar. For example, a blue and white *toile de Jouy* print in cotton looks good with a green and white cotton gingham, but if you used both a different color and a different fabric, such as green and white silk with the blue and white *toile de Jouy,* the contrast would be discordant and too emphatic. By repeating a type of fabric, you create an underlying harmony which counterbalances the contrasting effect of the color change.

Here, an apple green brushed cotton has been used on one chair and a bright emerald *toile de Jouy* on the other. The smaller sofa is upholstered in a simple lime green ticking and the larger one is covered in a wide stripe in moss green and white. Chambray blue has been used for a couple of the pillows and also for the checked sofa at the other end of the room. The blue forms a refreshing contrast with the green. Slip-covers have been used on much of the seating to continue the relaxed and informal atmosphere of the room. The white ground of the curtains keeps the scheme fresh and lively.

ABOVE *Blue and green are not commonly used together, but in this classic country house drawing room the combination works well, creating just enough contrast to add interest, without being dominating, as a stronger contrast of, say, red and green might have been.*

OPPOSITE *Delicate arching flowerheads of geraniums adorn the deep windows in this room, the pale pink flowers echoing pink tones in the pillows on the sofas, in sympathy with the floral motif of the curtains.*

Crackle-glazing a lamp base

This is an old technique that gives a wonderful antique finish to any paintwork, so that fine hairline cracks distress the appearance of the paint, resembling an old painting. Crackle varnish comes in a kit of two bottles: the aging varnish, which is applied first, and the crackle varnish, which is applied second. The reaction between the two causes the fine cracked lines to appear on the surface. You then need to rub a little dark pigment into the cracked surface to give it an authentically aged appearance.

you will need Sandpaper • Primer • Water-based undercoat • Base color such as green • Crackle varnish kit (aging varnish and crackle varnish) • Raw umber acrylic paint • Clear flat acrylic varnish

1 Lightly sand any existing paintwork, or prime the bare wood ready for painting with a suitable primer. Leave to dry, if using the primer, then apply one coat of the water-based undercoat.

2 Brush on the chosen base color of paint (green in this case) and allow to dry. You may wish to apply more than one coat of paint in order to give a better coverage of the lamp base.

3 Apply one coat of aging varnish and allow to dry for between 1 and 1½ hours. It should be faintly tacky to the touch, but not at all wet, and it must not dry completely. Then apply a thin coat of crackle varnish, and leave to dry overnight.

4 Rub a little raw umber (you can use raw umber acrylic paint if you wish) into the cracks, to give them an aged appearance. Leave to dry, then apply a single coat of clear flat acrylic varnish to protect the surface of the lamp base.

LEFT *In this light-filled view of the room, the subsidiary color scheme of mid-blue is carried out in the chambray blue check fabric of the sofa. The other colors form a contrast for the pillows. Gold-framed portraits provide additional warmth to the color scheme, in keeping with the country house atmosphere.*

RIGHT *Simple hand-sewn triple pleats are an effective treatment for these informal curtains. The use of a white ground for the fabric creates a fresh, and light look which is entirely suitable for this "gardenesque" room.*

The view of this study looks down the room, with the main window on the left-hand side. Surrounding it is a narrow green border, which helps to give definition to the window. The curtains fit neatly into the window recess, and the hand-sewn pinch pleats are decorated with large dark green chenille-covered buttons. The rich, soft colors—principally dark green, old gold, and burgundy, with a few hints of navy blue and ocher—are restrained and traditional. The mahogany furniture is in keeping with the overall look, which is redolent of country gentlemen's pursuits. The walls, papered in a dark green and sand check pattern, are subtle enough to mix with other patterns in the room, such as the paisley curtains and the rich red rug.

A Green Study

This rectangular room, which measures approximately 16 x 12 feet (4.9 x 3.7 meters), can double as a guest room cum office or as a study. It has been given a deliberately masculine character, both in the choice of colors and in the style of decoration. Dark green has long been a popular color, particularly in Victorian times when it was much in vogue for the dressing room attached to the master bedroom in large houses. It has a masculine, solid, and smart appeal and, of course, it goes particularly well with the rich brown of old mahogany which was such a favorite with the Victorians.

This study has undertones of the Scottish baronial feel, partly because of the dark paisley and splashes of tartan that have been used and also because it is a formal room with dark mahogany furniture and an overall masculine quality. The atmosphere in the room is enhanced by the period of the house (parts of which were built in the fourteenth century) and the deeply recessed windows and alcoves in the room.

This close-up of the bolster and pillows on the daybed reveals a rich mixture of colors and shapes. The ends of the bolster have been covered in the same fabric as the daybed itself, while the cylindrical section of the bolster has been upholstered in green chenille. A large button, also covered in green chenille, is the finishing touch for the end of the bolster, and continues the button theme of the curtains. The scalloped trim, which is made from felt, on the tartan pillow picks up another theme –the scalloped baize edgings to the shelves.

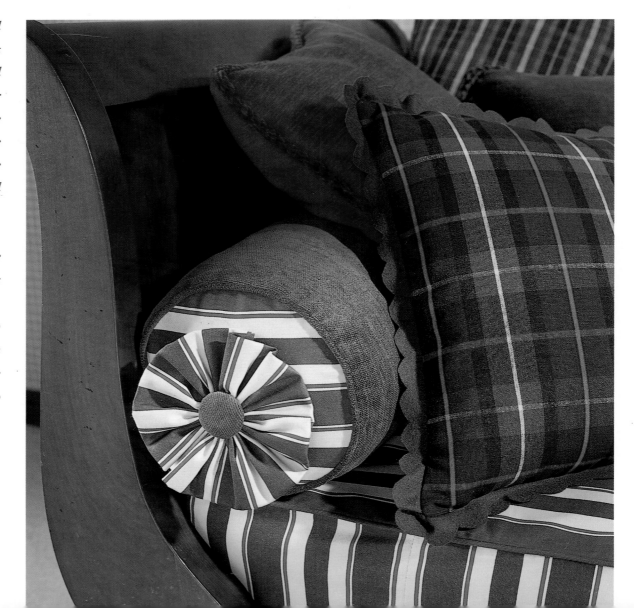

Dark green is extremely restful as a decorating color, but it usually needs a brighter contrast to give it life and warmth. In this room, sand and warm, rich burgundy have been used for this purpose, coupled with warm-colored, antique mahogany furniture. The walls have been papered in a simple green and sand check, and the carpet picks up the sandy color in the walls. The fabrics follow the theme of dark green, burgundy, and sand: the curtains are a beautiful, classic green and red paisley backed with a green Regency stripe fabric in dark green and burgundy on a sand background; the Queen Anne style chair is upholstered in dark green chenille with large red and green tartan patches, like the patches stitched on the elbows of a well-loved jacket; the seat of the upright chair is covered in the same tartan; and the daybed is upholstered in the green-striped fabric used to back the curtains. You could reverse the decorative scheme and use the wide green stripe for the wallpaper, with plain curtains with a sandy background for the curtains and upholstery, and the paisley fabric on the chair, but you would need to add more red as a contrast because the overall effect would be darker and heavier.

The fabrics gain much of their richness not only from the color but also from the rich texture of the weave. It is appropriate that these deep colors are used on a sand background because if they were set against white the contrast would be too jarring.

One of the unusual and most interesting features of this room is the way that different fabrics and patterns have been used to complement each other. The rich, deep green paisley curtains have been lined, luxuriously, with a patterned fabric that picks up the same colors in its simple, bold stripe. This adds elegance to the room. These dark, traditional colors form a wonderful backdrop for the collection of old books, school and college memorabilia, and sporting trophies that adorn the room.

Here you can see how two contrasting fabrics have been combined for the curtains, with the dark green, burgundy, and sand stripes creating the lining for the main fabric, a traditional rich paisley in the same colors.

Double-sided screen

Screens can be made from a variety of materials; this one is made from particle board in two hinged panels. One side is decorated with photocopies of antique maps; but old newspaper cuttings, left-over pieces of expensive wallpaper, or family memorabilia, such as letters, certificates, or school report cards, would be equally suitable. The weight of the papers should be roughly similar and ideally they should not be too thick. The other side of the screen is a simple bulletin board, made of baize criss-crossed with ribbon. The baize is secured with staples and the edges covered with strips of upholstery studs; these resemble single upholstery nails, but are much less time-consuming to use because the nails are not inserted one by one.

you will need

Proprietary primer • Maps, old newspaper cuttings, letters, etc. • Wallpaper paste • Sponge • Damp cloth • Clear acrylic varnish • Raw umber acrylic paint • Particle board screen• Green baize • Narrow ribbon • Staple gun • Strips of upholstery studs, and also single upholstery studs • Tailor's chalk

1 If you are making a screen yourself, prime it first with a proprietary primer. Apply wallpaper paste to the screen and the backs of the maps or paper. Position on the screen, carefully brushing out from the center. Check the edges are well glued, and smooth flat with a sponge. Wipe off surplus paste with a damp cloth. Leave to dry, then brush on a thin coat of varnish. Leave to dry. Mix a tiny amount of raw umber acrylic paint with a little varnish to make it runny, then add it to the varnish in small drops. Apply the varnish, leave to dry.

2 Measure the screen and mark out these measurements on the baize, allowing enough extra all around to cover the edges of the screen as well. Cut the baize slightly larger all around than you need. Stretch it over the screen and staple it in position at the sides with a staple gun, making sure that there are no creases or folds in the baize.

3 To finish off the sides of the screen in a decorative way, nail strips of upholstery studs down all the four sides, to cover the edges of the baize and the staples.

4 Measure a trellis grid for the ribbon on the screen with tailor's chalk. This particular trellis pattern has a 10 in (25 cm) distance between the ribbons. Fix the ribbon to the screen over the chalked lines with a single upholstery pin at each end, and at each intersection point of the ribbons.

A special finishing touch, which picks up the baize theme from the screen, is the scalloped decorative edging, cut from strips of green baize, for the bookcase shelves. To make this, you must first measure the length of the shelves. Then measure their depth and double it. Cut out a strip of baize to these dimensions for each shelf that will be edged. Of course, if the size of the shelves varies, you will have to measure each one separately. With ballpoint pen, felt tip, or tailor's chalk, mark the scallops along the long edge of the baize using an appropriate round object, such as a very small glass, as a guide. Carefully cut out the scalloped border with a pair of sharp scissors. Fix the edging to each shelf with a row of brass studs.

Decorative scalloped edging

One of the more novel uses of fabric in this room is the way that the arms of the Queen Anne style chair have been patched with a contrasting tartan fabric, in much the same way that the elbows of a favorite tweed jacket can be reinforced with leather when they start to show signs of wear. Although practical in inspiration, the patches can be purely decorative and will give a novel edge to a simple piece of upholstered furniture. Choose a fabric that coordinates with the main upholstery in color and pattern, but look for similar fabric weights and weaves–for example, do not mix cotton with silk. You could patch plain cotton rep with gingham, or a figured damask with a floral pattern in heavy linen union. With this chair, the colorways have a similar density of tone. This means that, although the patches are visible, they do not stand out too prominently–which they would if, for example, the tartan pattern contained white or an equally pale color.

The armchair patches

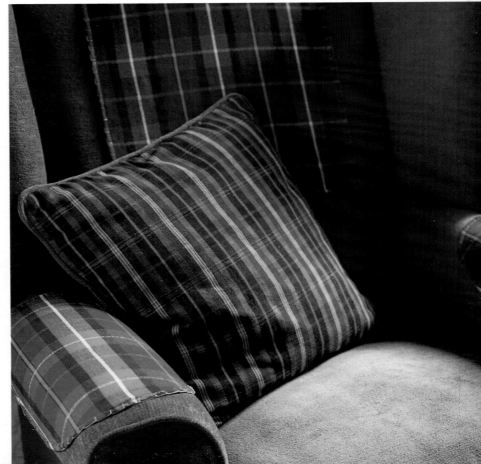

LEFT *The shelves on which the books are arranged have been edged with decorative baize scallops. This is a useful device for covering less than wonderful wood shelves or, indeed, white melamine shelves that are out of sympathy with the rest of a decorative scheme.*

RIGHT *This detail reveals the decorative blanket stitch around the edge of the patches on the armchair. This is for decoration only–any raw edges are best hemmed with zigzag stitch first to stop them fraying. You can stick the patches to fixed upholstery with double-sided adhesive tape, but they are easily stitched to loose covers. A contrasting tartan pillow picks out the tartan patches.*

Curtain treatments

There are several different curtain treatments in this room, partly because the room's three window recesses all vary. When planning curtain designs, it is important to take account of the scale and proportion of the windows and surrounding walls. In some cases, it is not possible to run a cornice across the window because it would take away too much light, or look ungainly. When there is little space, you are probably best advised to choose an attractive curtain heading with a neat, simple finish, as has been done here on one set of curtains with the hand-sewn pinch pleats, finished with buttons.

When it is possible to include a cornice, keep it in sympathy with the shape of the window and the overall feel of the room. Make sure that the weight and shape of the cornice suit the length of the curtains and also their thickness. A quilted and padded self-fabric cornice, edged with the lining fabric, has been used here to neaten and smarten the smallest window.

OPPOSITE *This view shows the very different styles of windows in the room. Although this is relatively rare in modern houses, it is a frequent feature of old houses, or where a couple of rooms have been knocked together. At the larger window, the curtains have been fitted neatly into the recess. At the smaller window, they hang outside it, topped with a self-fabric cornice.*

ABOVE RIGHT *The heavily padded and quilted self-fabric cornice runs across the top of the smaller window. A subtle but effective detail is the rolled and padded edging, used like a braid, in the wide green stripe of the lining fabric. This picks up and emphasizes the off-white in the paisley pattern.*

RIGHT *These paisley curtains have been given deep, hand-sewn pinch pleats, each pleat adorned with a button covered in dark green chenille for emphasis. The buttons provide a valuable color link with the dark green border detail surrounding the window recess. Small touches such as these make all the difference in a decorative scheme by pulling it together and ensuring that the overall effect is unified. This is important when several colors are used in one room, as they are here.*

CHAPTER 5

blues

Blue and white is one of the most popular color combinations. This attractive collection of pillows makes use of rich mid-blue and white in a range of patterns, with stripes and florals, checks and novelty prints mixed and matched in a variety of styles and shapes. The main pillow cover has been given a buttoned-on front panel–a quirky way to update a plain pillow.

Blue is one of the most relaxing colors of all. It is generally associated with tranquility and harmony, perhaps in part from its connotations with the sky and water, and color therapists advise us to wear blue when we are feeling under stress. The color range is enormous: the deepest midnight blues and ultramarines; regal blues such as navy, Prussian, and Windsor; denim; delphinium; deep sapphire; bright Mediterranean blue, cobalt, and cerulean; sky blue; cornflower blue; china blue; duck egg blue; chambray; ice blue; Wedgwood blue; forget-me-not blue; smoke; azure; Adam blue; and many others, including blues that are nearly purple (with plenty of red in their composition) and blues that are almost turquoise (with masses of green). For our purposes in this book, the color includes the more bluish mauves as well, such as lavender and amethyst. It is interesting to note how many of the blues we know are named after flowers. The pigment, blue, derives from three main colors–cobalt blue, ultramarine, and Prussian blue–all of which are fairly warm blues with a certain amount of red in them.

Among the first blue pigments were lapis lazuli, indigo, and woad. Lapis lazuli was very expensive, so was only used in paintings for the wealthy or for the Church. Indigo

and woad were two of the earliest natural blue dyes, both of which were obtained from plants. They were used extensively for dyeing wools and clothes. With the discovery of other pigments and minerals for paints and dyes, and also the invention of chemical dyes, the range of blues that were available grew considerably.

The vibrancy of blue shows up wonderfully in paintings, and many artists have used it to great effect. Lapis lazuli was used a great deal in the religious paintings and frescoes of the Renaissance, while more modern works of art use other shades of blue–Turner's seascapes were full of cold blues; Matisse's paintings used vivid, hot blues; Monet's series of waterlily paintings featured sea blues and misty lavenders; Dufy's watercolors of the French Riviera combined cool and warm blues; and Picasso is renowned for his "blue period." Blues used in the manufacture of porcelain, such as Wedgwood blue and the blues of willow pattern china, have also considerably increased the popularity of the color.

Like all colors, blue varies a great deal, not only

depending on the intensity of the hue and the tone or shade (see page 14), but by virtue of the color or colors you choose to combine with it. A combination of different tones of blue can look very effective, perhaps with small splashes of white, yellow, or another pale color to break it up. Alternatively, you could introduce a stronger, contrasting color that brings the blues alive. Colors tend to take on a different feel according to the other colors they are mixed with: if you put blue and red together, the blue will automatically look warmer; if you combine it with green, it will look cooler. In this way, you can change the effect of the particular blue you are using through careful choice of other colors, and you should be aware of this when deciding which color to put with blue. This is also an important rule to remember when choosing blue for a room that receives little light—unless you are careful about the particular shades of blue that you choose (using one that is very warm), and the other colors in the scheme, the finished effect can be very cold and unwelcoming.

Blue can be used for many different looks in the house, from the simple, rustic appeal of Mediterranean blue and white to much richer, deeper blues, combined with yellows, golds, or reds in an exotic, sophisticated combination. Particular shades of blue have special geographical or historical connotations—the Mediterranean blue mentioned above is a very clear, bright, pure blue which can stand up to the area's strong sunshine, while paler blues would look bleached out; a paler, cool gray-blue is frequently used in Scandinavian interiors; and Persian mosaics feature strong royal blues. A wonderfully rich turquoise is associated with Sèvres porcelain.

Fabrics

Blue is one of the colors used most often in fabrics, and frequently in geometric patterns—very successfully when combined with white or off-white in plain ginghams and broad stripes in various weights of cotton. Indigo is also one of the principal colors in the figurative *toile de Jouy* fabrics.

Deep navy blues work particularly well for velvets, chenilles, and damasks, as well as toiles, tickings, and ginghams. They can all look good when trimmed and edged in a contrasting, brighter color, such as emerald green or rich, ruby red. Many shades of blue create a fresh, sprigged look for country-style cottons, often on a white ground, and with the addition of other mid-tone colors, particularly yellows and greens, for a clear, spring-like effect. Provençal fabrics feature a lovely, warm blue, often combined with yellow and red. Blue Laura Ashley fabrics in such shades as sapphire, smoke, emperor blue, china blue, chambray, and classic navy are among the most popular in the entire range. They all look very fresh when combined with white, very pretty when used with pale pink, bright when combined with hot pink and lime green, and very rich when accompanied by golds, ochers, and burgundies.

Because of its color associations with water and the sea, patterns using blue sometimes have nautical or seaside overtones in novelty prints for quirky decorating–shells and boats are particularly popular. For the same reason, blue is often chosen for bathrooms, where a combination of blue and white is particularly successful because it looks so clean. The mid-blues that have quite a lot of red in their composition are much warmer and therefore much easier to use successfully.

Furniture

Blue is particularly effective when used for painted wood furniture. In France, for example, it is almost obligatory to paint your shutters that wonderful pale blue reminiscent of faded denims. Blue–in particular, a fairly deep, pure blue–can be used successfully to antique and distress wood furniture, which makes it an ideal color choice for an old pine hutch or simple kitchen cabinet. Much paler shades of a gray-blue have also been used a great deal in Scandinavian painted furniture, often with soft creams and a pale grayish-white. Smoky blue is particularly suitable for creating a Shaker look for paintwork and furniture. Try using it with a pale sandy yellow, rather than the sharper contrast of white. You could decorate a cottage kitchen in these colors, with a simple blue and white checked fabric and a hutch in distressed smoky blue.

Deep warm blues

The deeper, warmer shades of blue, such as navy, Prussian, Windsor, denim, and emperor blue, are generally based on two particular colors–ultramarine for paint dyes and indigo for textile dyes. These deep blues can be used over quite large areas: for wallpapers, perhaps, that combine the blue with a lighter color such as sand; or for fabrics, as upholstery on chairs and sofas or as curtains.

You need to find a complementary color to offset large areas of quite strong color. White is normally the chosen contrast, although such colors as yellow and plaster pink work equally well, according to the effect you wish to achieve. Navy, burgundy, and sand form another good combination. The color you choose will depend on the atmosphere you want to create, and on the amount of light the room receives. White will give a crisp, clean contrast, but yellow or orange may give a more unusual, contemporary effect and will really bring out the richness of the blue to make the room glow. For a very rich, smart and elegant room, you could use navy, burgundy, and gold.

Small areas, such as guest bathrooms and tiny kitchens, can be enhanced by painting or papering the walls in deep, rich blues–they go extremely well with warm mahogany

Simple, brilliant blue shutters against a plain white wall make a wonderfully strong color statement. This particular shade of blue—pure and warm—is one of the easiest to live with and combines particularly well with white. It succeeds in looking both modern and bright, but with a strong feeling of nature, no doubt from its connotations with the sea and the sky.

furniture, and will provide an excellent foil for blue and white china or other bright decorative elements, such as storage jars or cooking utensils in the kitchen. Try contrasting these blues with deep, rich reds, dark greens, and golds for the look of Victorian polychromy–the starting point could perhaps be a piece of maiolica ware in these three colors.

Mid-blues

If you opt for the richness of the Empire look, you can cover the walls in a mid-blue such as cobalt, cerulean, or deep sapphire. Self-toned stripes or a self-patterned damask-type paper provides a good background for showing off collections of paintings, prints, or china. Window treatments can be equally opulent in this color scheme, with swags if the windows are grand enough to take them, and perhaps fringes or tassels on the cornices or as borders to the curtains. A similar shade of blue can also be used for a simple, country cottage scheme, using plain cotton fabrics, rag rugs, and colorwashed walls. A bedroom in this vein might well have plain white linen on the bed itself, and white muslin bed drapes, or could look very contemporary with a wrought-iron bedstead.

The scheme can equally be inverted, painting the walls white or off-white, and picking out the woodwork–baseboard, chair rail, picture rail, and doorways–in the deepish mid-blue, with the upholstery and patterned fabrics in different tones of blue, mixed with one other color–brick red, perhaps, or peacock blue.

You can sometimes play successfully with different shades of blue, contrasting peacock blues (which contain a lot of green) with much warmer chalky blues, lavenders with turquoise, and so on. This could work successfully in a predominantly blue kitchen where simple kitchen furniture is painted in a range of blues, the room dominated perhaps by a lustrous, deep blue kitchen range. When playing with different shades of blue in this way, eschew white as a contrast and pick a complementary color with the same tonal values–a mid-green, perhaps, or a warm yellow.

Lighter, warm blues

Often associated with house-painting at the seaside, these blues–wonderful pure, powdery cobalt mixed with white in such shades as sapphire, deep powder blue, and azure–can form the core of many decorative schemes in a range of styles, from Mediterranean to colonial. Much depends on how and where these blues are used, whether for sophisticated self-striped wallpaper or for roughly painted stone. They make an excellent backdrop for the walls, doorways, and windows of country cottages, especially when combined with another color of matching intensity–perhaps a green or a yellow–for other items of furniture, whether they have been upholstered or painted.

Blue-greens

Cool blue-greens, such as duck egg blue, aquamarine, turquoise blue, Williamsburg blue, Wedgwood and Adam blue, need to be handled with care. They can look very cold and uninviting unless used in conjunction with warm-looking materials, such as wood, or combined with a warmer color, such as apricot or soft russet. Cream or off-white makes a less clinical contrast than pure white, and blue-green fabrics can sometimes look warmer in matt, woven forms than in shiny silks or chintzes. Blue-greens are often chosen for bathrooms, perhaps on the basis that, as they are reminiscent of the color of the sea they are the most appropriate choice. Painting in an old-fashioned flat paint would help to warm the color by giving it depth, as would combining it with warm-colored woods such as pine or oak.

Blue and yellow

This is a particularly attractive combination, because the colors are complementary in the color spectrum. As a result, the warmth of the yellow compensates for any inherent coldness in the blue tones, and gives them the life and zest they need. The combination of blue and yellow conjures up visions of summer wheatfields set against a deep blue sky. Blue and yellow has become a very contemporary color scheme. It was used a great deal in the 1980s when yellow became a popular color, and was partly inspired by the work of such artists as Van Gogh, who used these colors in a vibrant way.

Balancing the intensity of the blue and yellow hues is an important factor in the success of this kind of scheme–for it to work best, the intensity of each color must be of equal saturation, as in bright cerulean blue combined with sunshine yellow, or pale duck egg blue combined with pale primrose.

This color scheme also works well when one color is used as an accent. For example, you could choose deep sunflower or cowslip for the walls, with accents of delphinium blue as the pillows, curtain edgings, and lampshades.

When decorating a room in fairly equal amounts of two colors, such as blue and yellow, the aim is to ensure that the areas of color are equally balanced, so neither color predominates. Beware of arranging the colors too symmetrically, however, or they will look contrived. If you pick yellow for the walls, then use mostly blue for the furnishings, and use the yellow again for small touches such as pillows, chair seats, and curtain ties.

Blue and green

An old saying runs "blue and green should never be seen." Yet we do see the combination often enough in nature, and indeed blue flowers such as cornflowers and delphiniums are among the most popular of all. Gardens can be the inspiration for peaceful and relaxing country color schemes of blue and green, with touches of white or cream, particularly when combined in simple, floral patterns. For this kind of look, you could use mid-blues and mid-greens. The blues have a high proportion of green in them and the greens contain a strong element of blue, thereby creating a balanced match. Looking through gardening magazines and books will help you to find good matches of blue and green if you are in need of inspiration.

Blue and green are also used in Indian cottons and Provençal fabrics, with their evocations of wide landscapes, grassy swards, and relaxed informality. When used in conjunction with large expanses of white or off-white for the walls or floors, for example, the decor is given a fresh, almost seaside look. Another version of the blue/green color combination is dark blue with vivid emerald green, especially when other colors are included in the scheme to add more life–a golden yellow, perhaps, or a strong Indian red. This combination can be used to create a rich, opulent, Empire look with lustrous fabrics, embossed wallpapers, beautiful antique textiles, and gilded furniture.

Blue and pink

Blue and pink were especially popular in the eighteenth century, when a particular shade of powder blue was often combined with a soft pastel pink, frequently with gilded decoration. The style, known as rococo, was all the rage throughout Europe, and the combination of blue and pink was one of its hallmarks. The color scheme was also used on the Sèvres porcelain of the period, although the Sèvres blue was far more turquoise than pure blue. The circular closet at Syon House, in London, was decorated by John Fowler (of the design firm Colefax and Fowler) in precisely these sugar-candy pink and

In this pretty country room, the chambray blue walls form the perfect backdrop to the blue and pink drapes edged in blue.

blue shades, with the delicate detailing picked out in gold leaf. Another, less formal, scheme by John Fowler for a country bedroom combined blue and pink–the walls were given pale pink stripes, and the cornice of the pink silk curtains was edged with deep violet blue braid and tassels. The bedroom furniture was mahogany, and some of the chairs had blue and pink tapestry seats.

This softly contrasting combination of muted blues and pinks works particularly well for bedrooms, especially when teamed with slightly faded-looking floral patterns and delicately painted furniture. It goes well, too, with stenciling and stamping, and a smoky blue-gray works well with a soft, muted pink. In deeper tone, raspberry pink and a much deeper mid-blue containing a little red, such

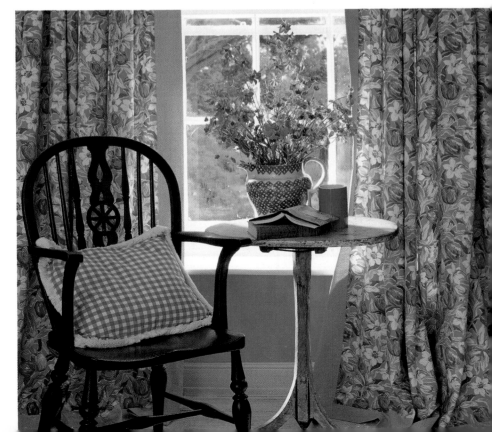

as a kingfisher blue, can be made to work well together, provided you use similar color saturations of each tone. The warmth of the raspberry compensates for any coldness in the blue, and could work well in a shady room, for example, where blue and white, the more classic combination, might look too cool and unfriendly. Raspberry and mid-blue combines well with deeper toned woods, such as rosewood and mahogany, in a more traditional look, with fabrics in thick damasks, chenilles, or velvets, and using more formal prints rather than pretty florals.

Blue and terra-cotta

Relatively recently, a very rich, warm, color combination of a slate-gray blue and brick red or terra-cotta became fashionable. It takes its emblem from the earth pigments of Mexico, in particular, and translates well into a simple design style, using rustic furniture, strong outlines, and relatively little pattern. With this type of color scheme, it pays to concentrate on surface and texture, as do the original colors in their native environment –roughly painted plaster and brick, and weathered and distressed furniture. This color scheme might work for a simple, unfitted kitchen or a hallway, combined with a natural terra-cotta floor. It might also work well in an informal bathroom.

Blue and white

The three colors from which blue pigment is derived–cobalt blue, ultramarine, and Prussian blue–combine extremely well with white, either as a contrast or to make a paler hue of the particular blue that is being used. This classic decorating combination of blue and white undoubtedly stemmed from its success in the decorative art of ceramics. Blue was one of the purest colors available as a glaze and therefore became popular all over the world.

OPPOSITE *Blue and white is one of the most popular color combinations of all. Here, a soft deep blue has been used for the wall of a clapboard house, while the ornate moldings of the woodwork have been picked out in white. Whether used for collections of china or in textiles, this deep blue, combined with white, is one of the most enduring color schemes because it is traditional yet looks fresh.*

In fact, the combination of blue and white is one of the most popular of all time, with some very famous associations. The inspiration for a lot of blue and white china is Chinese, dating from before the fifteenth century, and including such famous dynasties as Ming (which means "luminous" in Mandarin), featuring representational images in deep blue on a white ground. A variety of patterns and motifs was used, ranging from botanical designs such as acanthus leaves to animals and birds, all of which were symbolic. Islamic countries also began to produce their own designs of blue and white china, mostly in geometric designs on ceramic tiles. From there, the practice spread to Italy, where it featured in maiolica ware, then the Netherlands, where it is known as Delft china, and then to Britain.

When blue and white china arrived in Britain in the late eighteenth century, famous porcelain houses such as Worcester first made delicate blue and white tea ware in imitation of Chinese porcelain, complete with Oriental scenes and figures. In the following century, willow pattern china–a European design inspired by Chinese porcelain–was developed by such factories as Spode and became immensely popular. There was a profusion of blue and white transfer-printed china, including Spode's highly decorated Blue Italian design, which depicts a classical Italian lake scene. Indian designs were also popular, inspired by engravings and delicate botanical prints. The Wedgwood factory produced their own blue and white trademark, known as jasperware, which featured classical figures in white cameo relief on unglazed blue or other colored backgrounds. This followed the neo-Classical taste of the time, and was so sophisticated that rooms are still decorated in what has become known as Wedgwood blue, with paintwork, ceiling, and crown moldings picked out in white in the style of Robert Adam. Later came "flow blue," which has a darker blue glaze that literally flows over the outline of the transfer. It is very popular in the United States, as is the contemporary blue and white mottled enamel ware known as spatterware. Another rustic style of pottery is Cornish breakfast ware, which features simple, wide blue and white stripes.

When mixing blue and white, there are just as many designs and variations as in any other combination with blue, but certain themes are perennially popular. Stripes work particularly well in blue and white, whether in broad, even bands of chalky blue and white in such fabrics as muslin, sailcloth or canvas, or as dark navy and white ticking. Checks, such as ginghams, are also very attractive. The effect is clear, clean, modern, and simple, and combines well with other more elaborate representational patterns, such as blue and white *toile de Jouy* fabrics, and large blue and white cabbage roses in chintz or linen union. Fabrics and wallpapers featuring multicolored chinoiserie and botanical prints are often recolored and printed in a purely blue and white colorway. The original colors are replaced by varying shades of blue on a white ground to give a crisp and elegant design.

Blue and white tiles

The well-known landscape and seascape designs in blue on a white ground are immediately recognizable as Delft–the term used to describe tin-glazed ceramic tiles manufactured in the Netherlands in the seventeenth century. The tin glaze that made the distinctive Delft tiles–and their forerunners, sixteenth-century European maiolica ware–comes from adding tin oxide to the lead glazes that are generally used. This transforms the ordinary orange clay into the delicate creamy white ground that was used by the painters as a canvas for their brilliantly colored designs and that is such a hallmark of tin glaze ware. The deep, rich blue so characteristic of Delftware was formed by adding cobalt to the lead glaze. This technique was first used in southern Spain in the eleventh century, and a range of blue and white patterns is to be found in many countries around the shores of the Mediterranean.

One of the influences for Delft designs came from the Dutch East India Company's supply of Chinese porcelain, which was being imported from the Far East, and the resulting desire to create a cheaper, home-produced version. Civil war in China in the 1650s provided the trigger for massively increased production of blue and white tiles in Holland. The industry centered on the town of Delft, which is how the china came to be so named. The range of subjects used for the tiles extended into all sorts of naturalized objects, including flowers, animals, and scenes from everyday life such as boats and canals. The tiles were extremely popular outside as well as inside the Netherlands, and a thriving export industry developed. They are still popular today.

As the tiles were delicate, they were better suited for covering walls rather than floors. They were used in a whole range of applications, often as baseboards and to line the large, recessed fireplaces that were a feature of Dutch interiors of the time. Even whole walls were lined with Delft tiles, with the deeper blue tones accentuated by the paintwork on the door frames, window frames, and fire surrounds. The patterns and colorways so popular in tiles can be translated successfully into fabrics, using either patchwork or appliqué techniques, or can be stenciled onto painted surfaces, such as an occasional table or cupboard door.

OPPOSITE *Monet's house in France demonstrates a rich and exciting use of color, as befits one of the major colorists in the French Impressionist movement. Here, in this photograph of a corner of the kitchen, the warm tones of the copper cooking utensils make a rich contrast of texture and color against the cool blue and white tiles, and the blue and white kitchen cabinets.*

The rich, chestnut-colored floorboards in this light, cheerful family room provide a welcome warm contrast to the cool blue and white theme that forms the major decorating concept, based on the collection of blue and white china displayed on the hutch. The theme is taken up in the various fabrics, from the simple gingham chair seats, through to the antique toile de Jouy dress curtains.

A Blue & White Kitchen

This sunny family kitchen, with its huge bay window and river views, is part of an eighteenth-century London town house with an exotic history. During the days of the French Revolution, a French double agent lived here and was finally murdered on the doorstep. Today, the blue and white kitchen exudes an aura of warmth, friendliness, and light, is very much a living room too, and is the heart of a bustling family home.

The starting point for the blue and white scheme was the collection of china arranged on the hutch next to the window. The hutch itself has no particular claim to fame, and its simple white shelves have been given a facelift with antique lace. An equally useful device, if you do not want to use fabric, is to paint the wall behind the hutch in a plain, deep blue, which has the effect of making the china stand out in relief. The blue and white ceramic theme is extended in the decorative paint effects: a small rectangular panel on the lower part of the hutch has been stenciled in blue and white, using a design taken from a border on one of the china plates and which has been echoed on the mantelshelf edge over the fireplace. The motif on the blue and white tiles above the sink has been sponged behind the top shelves to continue the design.

As well as the collection of blue and white china, there is also one of Bristol blue glassware. To offset the simplicity of the glass forms, alternate shelves have been edged with strips of paper lace. Keeping the collection simple, and showing it off together, gives a wonderfully rich impression of deep, pure color that provides a much-needed contrast to the diffused color of the blue and white scheme.

The ceramic theme is continued through the choice of fabrics. A simple cotton, in a design inspired by Chinese porcelain, has been chosen for the curtains at the kitchen end of the room. At the formal end of the room, simple curtains have been made in antique *toile de Jouy*–there is no need to close them and the owner wanted to preserve as much of the view as possible, so they are dress curtains only. Mixing and matching pattern is also the theme for the blue and white pillows on the antique sofa. These have been created with overpanels which are either buttoned or tied to the basic pillow shape. The advantage of this type of construction is that you can create color changes by putting a different "bib" on the pillows if you wish, simply by tying or buttoning it on. Stripes, florals, checks, and even a novelty children's alphabet fabric have been combined in a range of permutations. This echoes all the different patterns in the collection of blue and white china on the hutch. A singularly pretty appliqué tablecloth, with breakfast motifs in the form of teapots, cups, and plates, has been made from scraps of the fabrics used for the pillows on the sofa. Directions for making this are given on pages 156–157.

The dining room chairs have upholstered seats that have been covered in upholstery-

OPPOSITE *Soldierly ranks of brilliant blue Bristol glassware have been lined up on the shelves, their orderly precision and solid, deep color offset by the pure white paper-lace shelf trimmings. You can often find old pieces of lace trimming that can be pinned to shelves to create this simple, but effective, edging.*

weight gingham, neatly self-piped with a double edge. A long settle on the other side of the table has been given a rectangular squab cushion, which is tied to the wooden seat at the corners with simple self-ties. Over the sink, the shelves have been dragged in light blue over a white-painted background.

Appliqué tablecloth

To make a tablecloth similar to the one shown, you will need a plain white damask cloth, along with some scraps of blue and white cotton fabric, in a variety of designs. You will also need a transfer fusing web, such as Wonder-Under, which can be obtained from any good notions department. The method shown is quick and easy but would not stand up to repeated washing, as the cut fabric edges would ravel. (For a more permanent design for everyday use, you would need to finish the edges of the appliqué motifs, either by zigzag stitching after applying them to the cloth or by turning under a seam allowance–which is added to the motifs prior to cutting them out–and slipstitching them onto the tablecloth by hand.) The steps below are for fusing the motifs to the cloth, without finishing the edges.

you will need White damask tablecloth • Scraps of several blue and white patterned fabrics • Small piece of plain fabric, for backing (not visible) • Transfer fusing web• Blue embroidery floss • Blue sewing thread

1 Draw a teapot on a piece of paper and cut it out. Place this template on a piece of plain fabric and cut around it. Iron a piece of transfer fusing web to the front of the fabric teapot, having first covered the ironing board with a piece of old fabric or paper.

2 Peel off the paper covering the transfer fusing web. From the patterned fabrics, cut out shapes to fit the teapot–the body of the pot, spout, handle, base, lid, etc.–and arrange them on the web-covered teapot like a collage. Iron the fabric shapes in position.

3 Iron another piece of fusing web onto the reverse side of the teapot. Iron this motif on to the center of the tablecloth. Using blue sewing thread, embellish the teapot with handstitches around the edges of the fabric shapes.

4 Appliqué cups-and-saucers and spoons to the tablecloth in the same way. Using blue embroidery floss, work running stitches to represent steam above each teacup, then embroider a scallop pattern around the edge of the tablecloth with running stitch.

Stenciling a design

BELOW *A plain white damask tablecloth has been given a new lease of life with appliqué motifs in blue and white. The blue and white china theme was inspired by the owner's collection of china shown on the hutch on page 161. You can create as many or as few appliqué motifs as you wish, stitched either by machine or by hand.*

To create a stenciled design from one of your own sources, you will need to be able to cut out a stencil yourself. This is normally done on oiled card (which is available from any art supplier), and you will also need a mat knife or other craft knife with a very sharp blade. Lay a piece of tracing paper over the design and trace over the outline with a soft 2B pencil. Then turn the traced design over, place it on the stencil card, and rub over the back with a hard object so that the image is transferred onto the stencil card. Place the stencil card on a cutting board and cut around the edge of the pencil line very carefully, using the mat knife or sharp craft knife.

To use the stencil, you will need to use masking tape to tape it to the object being painted, because this tape should peel off without marking the paintwork. If you are creating a border or repeating pattern, you will need to make registration marks (small holes) in the edges of the stencil so you can line up the pattern accurately as you move along the surface that is being painted.

To paint the stencil, you will need either purpose-bought stencil paints or regular latex. The paint must be fairly thick and not runny, otherwise it will run under the edges of the stencil and ruin the image. You will also need a short, stubby bristled brush called a stenciling brush. Mix or turn the paint into a tray and dip the stencil brush into the paint. Dab any surplus paint off the brush onto a piece of spare card, until the amount of paint on the brush no longer looks thick and blobby. Then, using an up and down motion of the wrist, pounce the paint through the holes in the stencil design. You may prefer to practice first on a spare piece of card if you are not used to stenciling, or want to check that you like the stencil you have made.

The stenciled design in this room was then picked out further with simple brush strokes and the border was painted in a deeper shade of blue for added definition.

RIGHT *A small stenciled border has been added to the front edge of the mantelpiece, the inspiration for it taken from the design on a china plate. Ornaments of all descriptions provide valuable source material for decorating concepts, whether in terms of color mixing or pattern making. The informal arrangement of white cottage garden flowers suits the relaxed mood of the room.*

LEFT *A neat frame of a blue and white ticking cornice and side covers has been given to the white hutch displaying the blue and white china. Frequently seen in Dutch houses, these simple fabric decorations for shelves and mantelpieces make an attractive addition to what is otherwise a simple piece of furniture.*

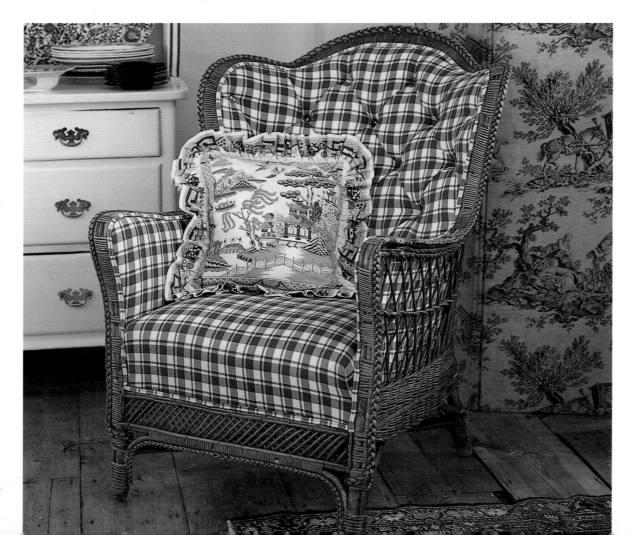

BOTTOM LEFT *Mixing pattern can have an exciting and uplifting effect on any decorative scheme. Here, a willow pattern design, echoing that of the china elsewhere in the room, has been employed for a ruffled pillow on this country-style wicker chair, upholstered and buttoned in blue and white check.*

RIGHT *The eclectic blue and white china collection, displayed to good effect against the plain white backdrop of the hutch, provides the inspiration for the mixture of colors and patterns in this room.*

This blue and yellow bedroom has a fresh, country appeal that derives in part from the color combination and in part from the use of simple cotton fabrics. While the chambray blue colorwashed walls provide the basis of the scheme, the touches of cowslip yellow—to frame the walls at ceiling and baseboard height, in the bedspread and the reverse and ties of the curtains—bring it to life and add a contemporary twist.

A Blue & Yellow Bedroom

In this room, chambray blue is combined with bright cowslip yellow. Each color has the same degree of saturation, which means that the two colors balance each other. This is an important aspect in the successful combining of strong, bright colors. The addition of yellow helps to give life and color to the blue. On its own, or combined with a less forthright color, the blue would tend to recede, even though it is quite strong. The blue here contains quite a lot of red, which pushes it toward the warmer end of the blue spectrum. The yellow also has red in its composition, which gives the two colors a unity and harmony they might otherwise lack. The same principle could be used with a more greeny yellow and a more yellowy blue. The addition of small touches of pink and purplish blue also emphasize the warm tones inherent in this color mixture. This makes it cheerful, friendly, and welcoming, and suits the simple charm of the furnishings and fabrics extremely well.

This room is fresh, simple, unpretentious, and youthful in appearance. The Provençal feeling of the room is created by the patchwork quilt and the use of gingham, as well as the choice of colors. The French theme is continued in the simple cotton used for the curtains—a bright chambray trefoil pattern has been used for the outside of the curtains, which are lined with the same trefoil pattern in cowslip; this is also used to make the curtain heading. Equally French is the subtle addition of hot pink picked out in the flowers, the pattern on the quilt, and some of the plates. A secondary theme is blue and white, used for the skirt for the dressing table, the trim over the mantelpiece, the bed skirt and the blue and white china.

This is a country room, yet it is also sophisticated in the way it combines color and pattern and in its details—a yellow border runs around the baseboard and another around the ceiling; scallops appear on the mantelpiece, bed skirt, and dressing table; and a valance shelf on which blue and white plates are displayed sits over the windows. All these decorative effects create a charming and timeless bedroom.

Colorwashed wallpaper provides a watery-textured background, contrasted with brilliant white paintwork and the bright cowslip yellow borders at both ceiling and baseboard height. These borders are an essential ingredient of the room because they consolidate the yellow theme without being overwhelming. Such borders are easy to paint: all you need do is fix masking tape to the wall, to give you a straight line to paint along and to mask off the remaining paintwork. When the paint is completely dry, you peel off the tape to reveal the colored border. If you wish, you can paint the contrasting strip around the edge of each wall, to create a paneled effect. An alternative to painting the borders would be to use a wallpaper border, which you might find easier to manage.

OPPOSITE *A rich tapestry of blue and yellow is created by the stripes of the cotton dhurrie on the floor, the blue chambray scalloped bed skirt and the deep yellow border of the quilt, set against the matching blue fabric of the dressing table skirt and the curtains beyond.*

Scalloped gingham trim

This fresh gingham mantelpiece trim with its piped, scalloped edge makes a charming background for ornaments in the same colors. You can adjust the size of the scallops to the dimensions of your mantelpiece. To do this, you simply decide the approximate size of your scallops, and divide this into the length around the mantelpiece (i.e. the front plus both ends) to get the number of scallops. If it is not a whole number, round the number up or down and divide it back into the length measurement. That figure is the exact width of each scallop, measured at the widest point.

you will need Fabric such as check gingham • Pair of compasses • Piping cord • Sewing thread • Fabric marker

1 Cut two strips of fabric to the total length around the mantelpiece (front plus both ends) plus ¾ in (2 cm), and to a width of half the width of each scallop plus 1 in (2.5 cm). Make a template—use a pair of compasses to draw the correct number of scallops as a line of semi-circles to the size you calculated. With a fabric marker, draw around the template onto the wrong side of one of the fabric strips, leaving ⅜ in (1 cm) between the scalloped edge of the template and the edge of the strip. With right sides together and raw edges even, stitch the two strips together along the scalloped line. Trim ⅜ in (1 cm) outside the stitched line, clip the curves, turn right sides out and press.

2 Cut 2 in (5 cm) wide bias strips and join them with diagonal seams, until you have a strip the length of the scalloped piece. Wrap the bias strip around piping cord and stitch close to the cord, using the piping or zipper foot on your machine. Cut a strip of fabric to the length of the mantelpiece plus 1¼ in (3 cm), by twice the depth of the mantelpiece plus 1¼ in (3 cm). Cut the strip so the patterns match when the scalloped strip is attached. Right sides together, pin the piping along one long edge and across half of each end of the strip, positioning it just inside the seamline, with the stitching ⅝ in (1.5 cm) from the edge. Clip into the seam allowance at the corners. Stitch.

3 Place the scalloped piece on top of the piping, also facing inward, matching the patterns. Pin and baste. Fold in half lengthwise, right sides together, and stitch along the seamline, ⅝ in (1.5 cm) from the edge, across both ends and along the long edge, leaving an opening.

4 Turn the mantelpiece trimming right side out, through the small opening you have left, and press. Slipstitch the opening, using a colored thread that matches the color of the mantelpiece trim, to close it. Fasten off the ends of the thread neatly.

These chambray curtains hang from a brass curtain pole. Their contrasting ties, in a cowslip colorway of the same fabric, echo the narrow painted border of cowslip yellow at ceiling height. The old valance shelf serves as a display shelf for a collection of antique plates.

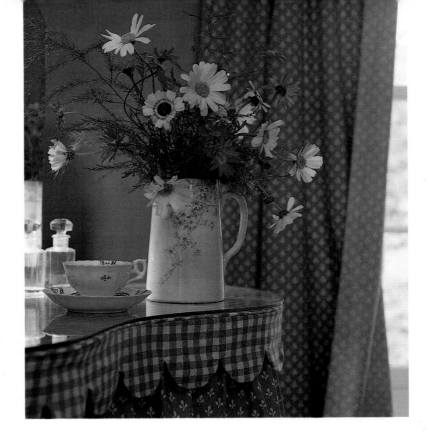

A simple vase of cottage garden flowers sits on the dressing table, whose scalloped edging in contrasting gingham makes an attractive contrast of pattern with the skirt below, and with the cowslip-colored lining of the blue curtains beyond. The use of a third color in the bright pink daisies and the central panel of the quilt (BELOW) accentuates and contrasts with the blue and yellow decorative theme.

An antique quilt with a central panel in a pink floral motif, echoed on the white bed linen, makes a splash of warm color in the center of the room. A similar antique quilt could form the starting point for a bedroom color scheme.

LEFT *A close-up of the window shows how the walls have been edged at baseboard height (as along the ceiling) with a narrow border of cowslip paint (the secondary color in the room), and echoed in the yellow reverse to the blue curtains. The three terra-cotta pots of pansies, in blue and yellow, pick up the theme.*

RIGHT *The rich pinkish blue of this hydrangea makes a vivid color statement against the similarly toned chambray blue colorwashed wall. The play of light and shadow on the flowerheads shows how texture, too, plays its part in our appreciation of color. The spongewear jug and the gingham tablecloth are classic country-style accessories.*

CHAPTER 6

reds

The use of red in history

For centuries, red was one of the more expensive pigments for dyes. It has always been considered a regal color–hence the phrase "rolling out the red carpet"–and was worn by royalty and heads of state. It was only in the late eighteenth century that synthetic chemical dyes were invented by the Georgians. Suddenly, they had a vivid new palette of colors to work with, and they swept away the muddy tones of the past in a magnificent display of bright, sometimes dazzling, colors. This coincided with a huge revival of interest in the architecture and decoration of Ancient Greece and Rome, and so the designers of the day began to use clear, jewel-bright colors in their decorative schemes. Red was one of these colors, and was especially favored by Napoleon. The "Gothick" gallery of Strawberry Hill, near London, was designed by Horace Walpole in 1776 and features rich red wallpaper which caused a stir when it was first seen.

Along with new shades of red, of course, came new shades of pink. Examples include the powder pink of the rococo style, soft pinks associated with Marie Antoinette, and rose Pompadour, which is a color made by Madame de Pompadour and seen in Sèvres porcelain. The combination of pale pink and warm, smoky blue was extremely popular in what became known as the Empire style, which developed in France in the late eighteenth century. One of the most famous examples of this style was Madame Récamier's bedroom, designed as part of a restoration by Louis-Martin Berthault of the banker Récamier's house. The walls were decorated with rich, violet-blue silk hangings, the bed was draped in white Indian muslin spangled with gold stars, and the paintwork was pale plaster pink and white. The room was visited by everyone interested in the new fashion in decoration. Another example of pink and blue, from roughly the same period, was the pinkish-red and mid-blue design for the music room of the house of the Director of the Royal Opera in Berlin. Deep pinkish-red panels, inset into plaster pink walls, were outlined in pale blue and the recessed alcove within them painted in blue and pink.

It was the Victorians who really popularized the use of red as it is known today. Red dining rooms and drawing rooms, as well as red hallways, were very much in vogue. The range of colors that were available continued to expand as more dyes were invented. Travelers returning from the Grand Tour brought with them such colors as Pompeian red, and the spread of the British Empire introduced exotic, spicy shades of red and orange. When Queen Victoria was made Empress of India, she had a room at Osborne House filled with her Indian possessions. Known as the Durbar Room, its color scheme was burnt red and white. Other popular color schemes, which are still in vogue today, included burgundy mixed with navy and bottle green. The abundance of pretty pink floral prints and chintzes that were produced are still classic decorating textiles.

OPPOSITE *Swedish style has become immensely popular, helped in part by the recent upsurge in interest in Swedish painters such as Carl Larsson (1853–1919), whose house this is. The wonderful combinations of orange-red with a deep inky blue and natural wood are not typical of the Swedish look but they do have the soft tint of color that is the hallmark of Swedish interior design. When the room was first painted in the 1890s, the color scheme did not meet with universal approval, to put it mildly.*

At its purest, red is one of the strongest colors in the spectrum. It attracts the eye and appears to advance upon you, so it is no accident that it should be the color used as a warning signal. Primary red is the color of fire and can have the same attributes—a brilliant, burning intensity. It is hard to be indifferent to red, as bold splashes of primary red are invigorating, dramatic, and full of zest. Interestingly, it is the color that small children seem to identify with most readily, perhaps because it is so visually arresting.

As with all the shades in the spectrum, red changes when it is mixed with other colors and when dark or light tones are added to it. It therefore covers a wonderfully large range of colors: from shell pink and rose to crushed strawberry and plum; from terracotta and plaster pink to crimson, cherry red, magenta, russet, and burgundy. Shades of red vary around the world. There are the spicy reds of India, the vermilions of Chinese reds, and the scarlets of Japan. Rich crimson is a color particularly associated with pre-Revolution Russia, with candlelit interiors glowing red and gold while the snow falls outside. In colonial America, reds were deeper and more somber, and many of the huge clapboard houses of New England were painted in these colors.

Hotter climates have more earthy and muddy shades of spicy red, which are mixed with yellow ochers and clay brown. Terra-cotta, brick, and plaster pink are often associated with Italy and come from pigments such as Venetian and sienna red, as well as the terra-cotta so abundantly used for roof tiles, floors, and urns. Plaster pink and brick are the colors of rough plaster and flaking stucco, and of the beautiful pink local stone which is used in decorative detailing on famous Venetian palazzos.

In Britain the Victorians introduced a national love of red, which became the color of many classic tourist symbols—including bright red mailboxes known as pillar boxes, scarlet telephone boxes, and the cherry red double-decker London bus. Red mixed with white produces pale pinks, and the exteriors of houses and cottages by the sea and in the countryside are often washed with these soft shades. One of the most charming associations with pink is the abundance of plants with pink flowers, such as roses, peonies, carnations, and old-fashioned pinks. They and other pink and red flowers have inspired generations of textile designers to produce chintzes, cottons, and linens abundantly decorated with floral prints.

Of all the colors in the interior decorator's palette, a pure, bright red such as pillar box red is the most difficult to use well. It makes an extremely strong statement, being both intense and vivid in hue, so any decoration scheme in which it is the major color needs to be thought through carefully, particularly if large quantities of it are being used. For this reason, it is usually best chosen for rooms other than living rooms and is often most

OPPOSITE *Red can be difficult to use successfully in interior decoration because it is such a strong and dominant color. When employed for small rooms that are not used very frequently, such as bathrooms or dining rooms, it comes into its own, especially when the color is relieved with interesting decorative surface patterning, as shown here.*

successful in dining rooms, where it creates a glowing atmosphere. The less pure forms of red—Indian reds, muted fuchsia pinks, terra-cottas, and russets—are softer colors and therefore much easier to live with, and will provide a successful color scheme in almost any room. That said, a strong, pure red can transform a room with less than wonderful proportions into an almost magical environment.

Pure reds

These colors are the primary reds, vermilions, and scarlets familiar to us through tomato red, hunting scarlet, and poppy red. When used as a major theme in decoration–as wall colors, for example–they provide the key decorative element to which all other colors play a subsidiary role. In other words, once you have chosen to paint or paper the walls bright red, you have made a commitment that will govern or even dominate all your other color choices in the room. This is not true of a less demanding color, such as blue, green or yellow, which will often provide a background to other colors. Red works well with other vivid colors such as yellow and bright green, and is particularly successful with white.

Red and white

The use of white as a contrasting color to a pure and strong red such as scarlet, vermilion, or crimson creates a fresh, appealing, and cheerful effect. It will also help to prevent the red from being too overpowering. Red and white gingham, stripes, ticking, country cottons, and red and white polkadot handkerchiefs–all with their connotations of rustic life–are appealingly clean-looking. They can look good with navy blue, if you want to tone down the brightness, and you can use off-white rather than pure white for a more muted contrast in color.

Red and white combinations work well for informal rooms, such as kitchens and children's rooms, as well as for bathrooms. The proportions of each color will affect the overall look–a mainly red room, with touches of white, will be rich, warm, and atmospheric, while a mainly white room, with touches of red, will be modern, fresh, and uplifting. Red and white can be warmed by the addition of indigo or sunflower yellow.

Red and yellow

Pure forms of red and yellow are sometimes difficult to use together as they can be too dominating, but they are a wonderful combination for a sunny Provençal or rustic kitchen, or even a child's playroom, when they can evoke the colors of red poppies growing in a field of corn. The combination of red and yellow also works well in the muddier shades of Indian red and yellow ocher. When deep burgundy and pale gold are combined, or rich tomato with old gold, the effect is extremely attractive. Using red as the predominant theme for the walls and the gold as a supporting color–for details and fabrics, perhaps–has been a major theme in many interiors.

Red and gold

With its connotations of royalty and majesty, a red theme can look sumptuous when combined with rich gold. The combination of red and gold was particularly popular when associated with velvets, brocades, and tapestries in both Renaissance interiors and in the Gothic revival of the Victorian and Edwardian periods. These "royal" colors of red and gold, along with imperial purple, instantly create a feeling of richness, wealth, and luxury, and often demand lavish drapes of fabric in detailed patterns. They can also be very successful when combined with deep blue, with cream, and with deep green for this Empire or Renaissance style, particularly when teamed with rich fabrics such as damasks, jacquards, velvets, chenilles, silks, and brocades.

A red and gold decorating theme can be used for bathrooms as well as for dining rooms and bedrooms. The gold element could be a pattern on fabric; trimmings or finishing details such as gold piping and gilded picture frames and mirrors; or gilded furniture. Small rooms will acquire an almost cocoon-like warmth and intimacy from the use of red, and it is often the ideal solution for a small, cold room which gets little light, as it provides an instant lift of vigor, and creates a warm, glowing atmosphere. Touches of gold will tone down the red.

This wonderful, rich, warm, brick-like color can be the most appealing of all the reds, and the easiest to use in decoration since it combines well with a wide range of other colors including gold, yellow, bottle green, cobalt blue, and turquoise in shades that vary from light to dark. Terra-cotta is a dominant feature in decoration all over the world. Based on natural earth and stone colors and the pigments of burnt sienna, light red, and Indian red, it varies according to the area in which it is produced and the minerals found locally, so can be browner if burnt umber or sienna is added, or more yellow if yellow ocher is added. In Mexico, a deep, rich, earthy terra-cotta is painted on the houses, and is often combined with sapphire blue as a direct contrast. Old Italian frescoes feature a wonderfully soft, pinky-gold terra-cotta, often used with dull gold, olive green, and white in color schemes that are well worth imitating.

In decorating, warm colors, like plaster pink and brick represent more subtle shades of terra-cotta. Brick can be a very smart color and is a more "neutral" terra-cotta color for downstairs decorating as well as for more masculine bedrooms. A warmer, redder shade of terra-cotta is russet, which is especially effective in traditional paisley and furnishing fabrics. Terra-cotta is one of the oldest forms of ceramic ware. Aged and weathered, it takes on a soft, warm character and its unglazed, undecorated quality has become immensely popular today for tiles and ceramics.

This marvelously ornate, Gothic-style room proves that a well-chosen red can add depth and warmth to large, open spaces.

Terra-cotta

Plums and burgundies

Deep, bluish reds, such as plum, cherry, claret, and burgundy, have a very distinct character, which is determined by the amount of blue added to the red and the darkness of the overall tone. They convey a feeling of autumn and winter, of fireside warmth and evening darkness, and were much used in Victorian times to produce a sense of solidity, security, and strength. Dark burgundy, which is the color of juicy berries, creates a calm, reflective atmosphere and therefore works well in studies and libraries. When combined with navy, dark green, sand, or gold, it is excellent for decorating downstairs rooms.

Today, these colors tend to be used in relatively small amounts, and often with one or more contrasting colors to offset the darkness–mustard yellows, mid-greens, and turquoises are all good choices. Dusty plum was a popular color in the Art Deco movement, especially when combined with pea green, and was also much used by William Morris in his textile designs. It enjoyed a big revival in the early 1970s.

Pink

Pink is made from combinations of red and white, sometimes with a little yellow or blue added, and ranges from the palest shell pinks, roses, powder pinks, and plaster pinks (which are sometimes almost neutrals because of the paleness of their tone), to the deep, strong pinks such as fuchsia, crushed strawberry, shocking pink, hot pink, and raspberry, all of which contain much less white and far more red. Being composed of lots of white, pink is a very fresh color. It is feminine, pretty and romantic, and is a marvelous color for

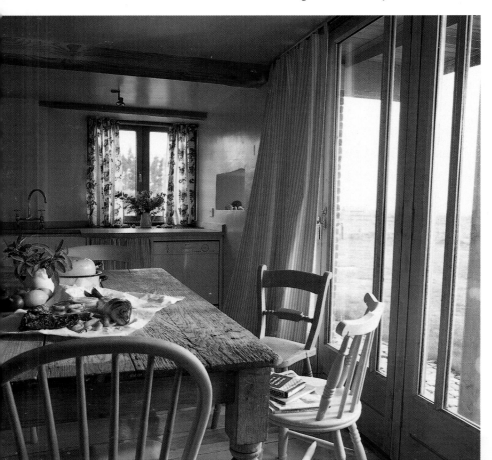

floral prints, from large splashy pink chintzes to simple country sprigs and faded linens. The colors reflect the pink flowers seen in gardens and so bring the garden into the home. For this reason, green is an ideal complement to pink in a decorating scheme because it represents the color of foliage.

In recent years pink has become an extremely popular color in the home decorator's repertoire, especially for living rooms and bedrooms, and is often combined with another color such as green or blue, and occasionally yellow. Rose and sapphire form a lovely, pastel combination, with raspberry and kingfisher blue making an effective stronger-toned mixture. Pink has long been popular as a colorway in floral fabrics, such as chintzes, linens, and sprigged country cottons, but has recently found a new vogue as a strong decorating color in its own

Soft reds and plaster pinks have been used for this large, light living room. When mixed with white as a contrast, red becomes much less oppressive. Combining reds, pinks, and whites is a novel approach to colormixing, and works extremely well in this mixture of Laura Ashley fabrics. The same living room has been decorated in yellow and white on pages 90–97, to show how much difference the choice of color can make to a room.

right, sometimes teamed with dusty yellow, teal, or smoky blue, and used in novel settings such as kitchens. Bright shades of pink are also used as solid blocks of color mixed with white, chambray blue, and apple green.

Muted pinks are some of the easiest colors to live with and they can add a great deal of warmth to a cold-looking room. Pale plaster pink, which is the color of raw plaster, is a very good "natural" earthy pink that is muted and less sugary than many pinks. It is a very popular 1990s color, which has been inspired by the interest in neutrals. In Italy and India, dusty, rather faded pinks such as old rose are very popular as a principal decorating color, often to colorwash both interior and exterior walls.

Hot pink, shocking pink, deep pink, and crushed strawberry are also excellent decorating colors, especially when used as an accent color that brings depth to a pale room. These shades are soft yet full of impact, cheerful and sometimes quirky without being overpowering as primary red can be. They are also good accent colors in multi-colored floral prints as well as being used plain on upholstered surfaces.

Pink, and especially old rose, is fabulous for a romantic country house style bedroom, with sheer voile drapes and pink chintz fabrics. Pink can look antique and timeworn on linens lightly dyed with tea, and soft country tones can be used for a relaxed, yet elegant living room. Pink can be exuberant and arresting in deeper tones for modern, simple schemes with splashes of bright color for a dramatic, smart downstairs room.

OPPOSITE *This seaside kitchen has been painted in a pale shell pink, which gives it a light and spacious feel. Candy-striped ticking has been used for the simple tab-headed curtains, while a novelty 1950s print provides an element of eccentricity at the smaller window. The kitchen chairs, which are all different, have had their dissimilarity emphasized with an individual, but toning, paint treatment –lichen and ointment pink are among the colors.*

This view of the red dining room from the door demonstrates its richness of contrast, the deep warm ruby red of the walls providing an enclosing cocoon for the central focus—the dining table—with its array of gold-plated china and sparkling crystal. Texture is a key element here—with the woven fabrics and the walls providing the warmth, contrasted with the sharp brilliance of the gilded crown moldings, curtain pole, and mirror, and the pure white expanse of the damask tablecloth.

A Red Dining Room

This rich, luxurious dining room uses glowing Indian red to great effect as the major element in the color scheme. It transforms a functional room into one with a particularly strong character and in which dark colors play the dominant role. Such an obvious color statement might be too overpowering in a living room or bedroom, but it is possible to do this in a dining room because red is an ideal color for a special room that is not used everyday, especially if it comes to life at night. When combined with candlelight bouncing off the gilding, glassware, and textured walls, red creates a marvelous, glowing atmosphere. Although the architecture of this room, with its high ceilings, lends itself well to this kind of elegant, sophisticated, and formal style, this scheme would work equally well in a smaller room.

The essence of this decorative scheme is the color and texture of the walls, which have been colorwashed in two shades of red. Colorwashing is particularly effective in this context, where different shades of red are used because, instead of the flat finish that a plain color provides, colorwashed walls reflect light.

An important touch in this room is the antiqued gilding of the crown moldings, which helps to create the rich look while adding a further glow to the room. Covering the dining table, which forms a large expanse in the center of the room, is a sparkling white damask cloth which creates a contrast of tone that is further enhanced by the off-white marble of the fireplace surround and the off-white painted ceiling.

Another element that lifts the overall color scheme and acts as a counterpoint to the deep red because of their light-reflecting qualities is the use of mirrors and glass. The large mirror over the fireplace, with its gilded frame, bounces back reflections from the window, while the chandelier and the glasses on the table also pick up these reflections.

The chenille curtains create a suitably Renaissance feel, partly from the combination of the classic colorway of navy, burgundy, and old gold, and partly from the broad stripes. These have been created by stitching panels of the different fabrics together, then emphasizing the seams with braid in the same three colors. This is relatively simple to do, and creates an individual touch to the room. Interlining the curtains with extra-thin batting gives them the appearance of rich Renaissance wall hangings and the three stripes make them look like beautiful flags. It is worth noting that in designing these striped curtains, the stripes were cut in proportion to the window. These curtains give weight and emphasis to the window, as a contrast to the darkness of the walls. The undershade, made from an elegant woven jacquard in old gold through which the light can pour, also helps to brighten the overall effect.

The dining chairs have also been covered in a woven jacquard in the same colors as

OPPOSITE *Woven pattern is at the heart of this combination, as these chairs upholstered in a gold and burgundy jacquard and the figured damask tablecloth demonstrate. By reversing the fabric treatment on the chairs, using one colorway for the front and another for the chair back and seat, with contrasting welting, attention is drawn to the pattern of the fabric.*

those used for the curtains, but with a twist. A floral, elegant gold-colored jacquard has been used for the chair backs, while the seats and reverse of the chairs have been covered in the burgundy colorway, and piped in navy cord. This reflects the three colors used in the curtains. If your dining chairs are not upholstered, you could still copy this idea by making loose covers for them and combining the fabrics in a similar way. The burgundy and gold theme is echoed in the fitted cover for the armchair by the window, which is covered in the same gold jacquard as the chair backs and given a burgundy chenille cushion to create a lavish but elegant and sophisticated atmosphere.

Gilded pole

You can use various methods for gilding, including a very good gilding cream which can be bought in several shades in small pots. It is fairly expensive and if you are gilding a large area, as here, then you will find it less costly to make up your own gilding paint from bronze powder and polyurethane varnish. You can buy the bronze powder at any specialist paint supplier.

you will need   Sandpaper • Mineral spirits or rectified turpentine (optional) • Latex-based paint in dark maroon • Bronze powder • Polyurethane varnish

1 When gilding a curtain pole, you need to decorate not only the pole itself but also its component parts—the finials and the supports.

2 Sand back the pole to remove any varnish or stain, and then clean the sanded surface with mineral spirits or rectified turpentine to neutralize it. (If you use one of the newer furniture paints in Step 3 you can omit this step—most of the paints will cover varnished wood, but check the directions on the can first.)

3 Paint the pole with latex-based paint to prime it, ideally in a dark maroon color. Here, alizarin crimson acrylic paint was mixed with a little Prussian blue acrylic paint to tint a latex base, but a deep reddish-brown purpose-bought flat water-based furniture paint or household latex will serve the same purpose.

4 Mix a teaspoonful of bronze powder with polyurethane varnish, and then stipple this medium onto the pole with a stiff brush, making sure you do not overload the brush. Aim to create an uneven, mottled finish, so that the base coat shows through. Leave to dry for 24 hours and then give the pole a coat of polyurethane varnish for protection.

LEFT *Deep blue, red, and gold are the principal colors of these Oriental-inspired antique cups and saucers. Attractive and colorful ceramics can often form the inspiration for a particular color scheme, which is then expanded to encompass the furnishings in the room.*

RIGHT *Crystal glassware has a special ability to reflect light, while the arrangement of deep red roses and blue anemones in the center of the table picks up the color theme of the room. The trailing stems of ivy add a contrast of color and introduce a note of informality.*

ABOVE *The uneven color and texture of the paint effect on the walls gives them life and warmth which a flat, uniform color does not provide. The secret is to apply two or three diluted coats that are tonally similar, giving a depth and density of hue which contrasts beautifully with the gilded crown molding.*

RIGHT *Texture plays an important part in the way we perceive color. Here, the glossiness of the fruit contrasts with the more matte texture of the walls behind, while the glow from the mahogany table matches the sheen on the porcelain dish. The white and blue of the glaze make a dramatic contrast with the deep tones of the red.*

A warm glow suffuses this bathroom, with its rich and eclectic mixture of color and texture. The warm terra-cotta colorwashed and white-stenciled walls are the dominant feature, seconded by the informally draped red check curtains at the large window. Antique and ethnic furniture takes the place of standard fitted bathroom cabinets, giving this large bathroom an exotic character with a relaxing style.

A Terra-cotta Bathroom

BELOW *A slender wrought iron pole, with attractively curved finials, makes a suitable support for these simple check curtains, held in place with metal rings.*

OPPOSITE *A yellow, bright pink, and orange Madras check cotton is used again to create a skirt for the basin. Its design was inspired by a beach windbreak, and it was made from an old towel rack.*

Conjuring up images of India in the colonial era, this eccentric bathroom has an almost tentlike feel to it–warm, enclosing, and secure. Ethnic and colonial chairs and cupboards, informal check pillows, and Indian throws have all been used in this large bathroom to give it an informal, comfortable, and quirky character. The old claw-foot bathtub, and the texture and warmth of the pine floorboards, give the room a lived-in, familiar quality despite the exotic decorating scheme.

Touches of white bring the terra-cotta to life and make it less intense while also picking up the white enameling from the bathtub and basin. The stenciled pattern on the walls, inspired by Indian woodblocks, has been created in broad stripes, using three different stencils. This is a very successful way of creating an irregular, spontaneous pattern. The white ceiling and white picture rail help to define and enclose the pattern. The mix of terra-cotta with turmeric, and other spice colors also brings warmth and life to the room because they are not perfectly coordinated colors but an eclectic mix, and so create a relaxed and natural feel.

Generous amounts of brightly colored Madras check cotton at the windows–in a different, deeper, and purer red than that used for the walls–help to make the bathroom less formal, as does the lack of tiling or other hard surfaces that are so commonly used in bathrooms. The sides of the white enamel bathtub have been painted in deep red, while the plain white enamel basin has been given a wooden surround, inspired by a seaside windbreak, covered in a strong yellow Madras check.

This style of bathroom, with only minimum attention paid to the function of the room, is ideal for adults, but less suitable for a family bathroom where large quantities of water will probably find their way onto the walls and floor. It would also work very well, on a smaller scale, for a bathroom adjoining a master bedroom in which the colors were reversed, with white being the principal color and Indian red and warm golden browns the secondary colors.

The scheme shows how a bathroom can be far more than a purely functional room, and you can devise a really dramatic scheme. This bathroom is particularly interesting for displaying the owner's collection of ethnic artifacts collected from their travels. A scheme like this would work equally well in a kitchen or dining room.

Braided rag rug

A simple, braided rug can be made up from strips of leftover fabric—cottons, wools, or whatever you have to hand. However, it is best not to mix the types of fabric in one rug, and it looks nicer if you limit the color palette to a range of three or four colors, and tones of these colors. Part of the charm of this rug comes from seeing the raw edges of the fabric strips, but if you prefer a smoother, harder-wearing finish, the strips should be cut to twice the width of these and the edges folded in to meet in the center; the strips are then folded in half. (A proprietary trimming-and-tapemaking tool makes the job easier.)

you will need   Selection of fabrics • Strong thread

1 Tear up strips of fabric into lengths roughly 1½ in (4 cm) wide. Knot three pieces of fabric together at one end and pin the knot to a stable surface. Braid the fabric.

2 When you reach the end of a strip, hand-sew a new strip to it, overlapping the ends. (An even quicker, but less hard-wearing method is simply to wrap the end of the new strip around the old one.) Continue until the braid is several yards (meters) long.

3 Now begin coiling the braid into a circle, hand-sewing the coils together on the reverse side. (If you are using wider, folded strips, the traditional method is to lace adjacent coils together invisibly.) When you have coiled the entire braid, join on more strips and braid them together, then continue coiling the braid and sewing it together.

4 When the rug is the size you want, taper the strips and oversew the end of the braid to secure it and stop it raveling. Tuck the end under the adjacent coil and sew in place. Neatly sew in the ends of the thread, then trim them so no loose ends are visible.

LEFT *The rich colors of the curtain fabric need no further adornment. Simple tie-backs made from a strip of the same fabric keep the curtains in position, while the pattern-mixing theme is taken up in the ethnic quilt thrown over the back of a planter's chair.*

RIGHT *A framed Indian print, the ethnic cupboard, and the small wooden box help to create the inspiration for this bathroom. A mixture of freehand painting and stenciling, drawn from Indian woodblock designs, has been used here to create a repeating sequence of three different stripes on the terra-cotta washed walls.*

Laura Ashley Shops

UNITED STATES OF AMERICA
Albany 518 452 4998
Ann Arbor 313 747 6620
Ardmore 610 896 0208
Arlington 703 415 2111
Atlanta-Lenox 404 231 0685
Atlanta-Perimeter
    404 395 6027
Austin 512 451 4036
Bal Harbor 305 864 5628
Beachwood 216 831 7621
Birch Run 517 624 9297
Birmingham 205 985 0090
Bluffton 803 837 4339
Boca Raton 407 368 5622
Boston 617 536 0505
Bridgewater 908 725 3700
Buffalo 716 681 8600
Burlington/Boston
    617 272 4540
Burlington/Vermont
    802 658 5006
Carmel-by-the-Sea
    408 624 8095
Central Valley 914 928 4561
Charleston 803 723 3967
Charlotte 704 362 0926
Charlottesville 804 971 7707
Chattanooga 615 855 5496
Chestnut Hill 617 965 7640
Chicago 312 951 8004
Cincinnati 513 793 5535
Columbus 614 224 5057
Corte Madera 415 924 5770
Costa Mesa 714 545 9322
Cranston 401 946 1211
Dallas-Galleria 214 980 9858
Danbury 203 790 5068
Dayton 513 299 9007
Denver-Cherry Creek
    303 322 9401
Des Moines 515 243 8881
Destin 904 654 9771

Edina 612 920 2811
Fairfax 703 352 7960
Farmington 203 521 8967
Fort Lauderdale 305 563 2300
Fort Worth 817 346 4666
Freeport 207 865 3300
Germantown 901 756 7036
Gilroy 408 848 5470
Glendale 818 242 0428
Grand Rapids 616 942 6828
Greenville 302 575 1653
Greenwich 203 661 5678
Grosse Pointe 313 886 6960
Hackensack 201 488 0130
Hingham 617 740 4122
Honolulu 808 942 5200
Houston 713 871 9669
Houston/West Oaks
    713 558 6113
Indianapolis 317 848 9855
Jacksonville 904 358 7548
Jeffersonville 614 948 2019
Kansas City 816 931 0731
King of Prussia 610 354 9130
Knoxville 615 558 6385
Lake Forest 708 615 1405
Lancaster 717 397 7116
Lexington 606 253 1724
Little Rock 501 666 0272
Los Angeles 310 553 0807
Louisville 502 585 2424
Manhasset 516 365 4634
McLean 703 827 0074
Miami 305 233 8911
Milwaukee 414 347 1930
Minnetonka 612 546 4613
Montgomery 205 284 7011
Myrtle Beach 803 236 4244
Nashville 615 383 0131
New Haven 203 782 9436
New Orleans 504 522 9403
New York City/Westside
    212 496 5110

New York City/57th Street
    212 752 7300
Newport 401 846 6980
North Bethesda 301 984 3223
Northbrook 708 480 1660
Novi 313 348 9260
Oakbrook 708 572 9195
Oklahoma City 405 848 6252
Omaha 402 390 2085
Orlando 407 351 2785
Osage Beach 314 348 1333
Owings Mills 410 363 2455
Palm Beach 407 832 3188
Palm Beach Gardens
    407 624 5901
Palm Springs 619 322 2099
Palo Alto 415 328 0560
Phoenix 602 956 6043
Pittsburgh 412 367 8881
Pittsburgh 412 621 0735
Pleasanton 510 463 8714
Portland 503 224 0703
Prince William 703 474 3124
Princeton 609 683 4760
Raleigh 919 781 1076
Reading 215 373 5495
Redondo Beach 310 542 4436
Richmond 804 740 1406
Ridgeland 601 957 9063
Rochester 507 287 1073
Sacramento 916 923 5696
Salt Lake City 801 363 8408
San Antonio 512 377 2833
San Diego 619 234 0663
San Diego 619 452 6116
San Francisco 415 788 0190
San Marcos 512 396 5570
Santa Ana 714 834 1211
Santa Barbara 805 682 8878
Santa Clara 408 244 3551
Scarsdale 510 947 5920
Schaumberg 708 619 9110
Seattle 206 343 9637
Secausus 201 863 3066

Short Hills 201 467 5657
Skokie 708 673 6604
Southampton 516 287 2104
Stamford 203 324 1067
Stony Brook 516 689 6622
St Augustine 904 823 9533
St Louis 314 993 4410
Tampa 813 253 2177
Towson 410 825 0362
Troy 810 649 0890
Tulsa 918 749 5001
Walnut Creek 510 947 5920
Washington 202 338 5481
Westport 203 226 7495
Williamsburg 804 229 0353
Williamsburg 319 668 1555
Winston Salem 919 760 3733
Winter Park 407 740 8900
Woodbury 516 367 2810
Woodland Hills 818 346 7560
Worthington 614 433 9011

MOTHER AND CHILD
STORES
Birmingham 205 987 7566
Chestnut Hill 617 965 5687
Denver-Cherry Creek
  303 322 9403
Farmington-Hartford
  203 561 4870
Hackensack-Riverside
  201 342 1222
Houston 713 622 2262
Kansas City 816 931 2810
King of Prussia 610 354 9137
Princeton 609 683 1300
Redondo Beach 310 542 6228
Schaumberg 708 240 1910
Short Hills 201 467 5657
Stamford 203 359 9902
Tulsa 918 749 5063
Walnut Creek 510 947 3932

HOME FURNISHING
STORES
Alexandria 703 739 2144
Ardmore 215 896 8293
Atlanta 404 842 0102
Boston 617 357 5151
Burlingame 415 344 1774
Costa Mesa 714 545 7927
Dallas 214 691 6871
Kansas City 816 531 8971
New York City 212 735 5000
Ridgewood 201 670 0868
Short Hills 201 564 9600
Washington 202 686 1200

UNITED KINGDOM
LONDON SHOPS
Brent Cross (clothes only)
  0181 202 2679
Chelsea 0171 823 7550
Covent Garden 0171 240 1997
Ealing 0181 579 5197
Kensington 0171 938 3751
Knightsbridge (clothes only)
  0171 823 9700
Knightsbridge (home
  furnishings only)
  0171 235 9797
Marble Arch 0171 355 1363
Oxford Circus 0171 437 9760

COUNTRY SHOPS
Aberdeen 01224 625787
Aylesbury 01296 84574
Banbury 01295 271295
Barnet 0181 449 9866
Bath 01225 460341
Bedford 01234 211416
Belfast 01232 233313
Beverley 01482 872444
Birmingham 0121 631 2842
Bishops Stortford
  01279 655613

Bournemouth (clothes only)
  01202 293764
Brighton 01273 205304
Bristol, Broadmead
  0117 922 1011
Bristol, Clifton 0117 927 7468
Bromley 0181 290 6620
Bury St Edmunds
  01284 755658
Cambridge 01223 351378
Canterbury 01227 450961
Cardiff 01222 340808
Carlisle 01228 48810
Chelmsford 01245 359602
Cheltenham 01242 580770
Chester (clothes only)
  01244 313964
Chester (home furnishings only)
  01244 316403
Chichester 01243 775255
Colchester 01206 562692
Derby 01332 361642
Dudley 01384 79730
Eastbourne 01323 411955
Edinburgh (clothes only)
  0131 225 1218
Edinburgh (home furnishings
  only) 0131 225 1121
Epsom 01372 739595
Exeter 01392 53949
Farnham 01252 712812
Gateshead 0191 493 2411
Glasgow 0141 226 5040
Guildford 01483 34152
Harrogate 01423 526799
Heathrow 0181 759 1951
Hereford 01432 272446
High Wycombe 01494 442394
Hitchin 01462 420445
Horsham 01403 259052
Ipswich 01473 216828
Ipswich 01473 721124
Isle of Man 01624 801213
Jersey 01534 608084

Kings Lynn 01553 768881
Kingston 0181 549 0055
Leamington Spa 01926 314584
Leeds 0113 245 0622
Leicester 01162 513165
Lincoln 01522 511611
Llanidloes 01686 412557
Maidstone 01622 750138
Manchester 0161 834 7335
Middlesbrough 01642 226034
Milton Keynes 01908 660190
Newcastle-Under-Lyme
  01782 662014
Newport I.O.W. 01983 821806
Northampton (clothes only)
  01604 231975
Norwich 01603 632958
Nottingham 01159 503366
Oxford 01865 791689
Perth 01738 623141
Peterborough 01733 311766
Plymouth 01752 268344
Preston 01772 202425
Reading 01734 594313
Richmond 0181 940 9556
Salisbury 01722 338383
Sheffield 0114 270 1855
Sheffield Meadowhall
  0114 256 8221
Shrewsbury 01743 351467
Skipton 01756 700301
Solihull 0121 704 4344
Southampton 01703 228944
Southport 01704 546214
St Albans 01727 864611
Stockport 0161 474 7927
Stratford-Upon-Avon
  01789 298852
Sutton 0181 643 9790
Sutton Coldfield
  0121 355 3671
Swindon 01793 641727
Taunton 01823 288202
Tenterden 01580 765188

Torquay 01803 291443
Truro 01872 223019
Tunbridge Wells 01892 534431
Watford 01923 254411
Wilmslow 01625 535331
Winchester 01962 855716
Windsor (clothes only)
  01753 854345
Windsor (home furnishings
  only) 01753 831456
Worcester 01905 20177
Worthing 01903 205160
Yeovil 01935 79863
York 01904 627707

REPUBLIC OF IRELAND
Cork 00 3532 127 4070
Dublin 00 3531 679 5433

HOMEBASES
Within Sainsbury's Homebase
  House and Garden Centers
Basildon 01268 584088
Basingstoke 01256 469510
Bath 01225 339293
Blackheath 0181 856 9767
Bradford 01274 611929
Branksome 01202 768311
Brentford 0181 847 2214
Camberley 01276 686227
Cardiff 01222 499675
Catford 0181 461 0606
Chelmsford 01245 257257
Chichester 01243 533373
Colchester 01206 869187
Coventry 01203 715901
Crawley 01293 538351
Crayford 01322 558614
Croydon 0181 684 8250
Derby 01332 291260
Enfield 0181 366 2236
Gloucester 01452 526806
Guildford 01483 304115
Harlow 01279 413355

Hatfield 01707 275837
Hendon 0181 200 7737
Hull 01482 572434
Ilford 0181 590 0212
Ipswich 01473 721124
Kensington 0171 603 2285
Kingston 0181 949 7861
Leeds 0113 268 5010
Leicester 0116 254 6075
Luton 0582 593445
Maidstone 01622 715400
Mill Hill 0181 203 7740
Milton Keynes 01908 692727
New Southgate 0181 368 1698
Newcastle-Under-Lyme
  01782 711752
Northampton 01604 234143
Norwich 01603 417474
Nottingham 0115 941 3885
Oldbury 0121 544 7333
Orpington 01689 890353
Oxford 01865 747979
Penge 0181 778 4214
Rayleigh Weir 01268 745374
Reading 01734 584572
Richmond 0181 876 2235
Rochester 01634 200088
Romford 01708 730326
Sheffield 0174 255 5175
Southampton 01703 510098
Stockport 1061 474 7489
Swansea 01792 650935
Swindon 01793 487125
Tunbridge Wells 01892 546646
Wakefield 01924 387011
Walsall 01922 29524
Walsgrave 01203 602086
Waltham Cross 01992 625275
Walthamstow 0181 531 8233
Watford 01923 252075
Willesden 0181 459 3989
Wimbledon 0181 946 9802
Worcester 01905 420401
Worle 01934 512628

York 01904 643911

CANADA
Willowdale 416 223 9507
Calgary, Alberta 403 269 4090
London, Ontario 519 434 1703
Montreal 514 284 9225
Ottawa 613 238 4882
Quebec 418 659 6660
Sherway Gardens, Etobicoke
  416 620 7222
Toronto 416 922 7761
Toronto-Yorkdale
  416 256 2040
Vancouver 604 688 8729
Winnipeg 204 943 3093

AUSTRIA
Graz 0316 844398
Innsbruck
  0152 579254/579257
Linz 070 797700
Salzburg 0662 840344
Vienna 01 5129312

BELGIUM
Antwerp 03 2343461
Bruges 050 349059
Brussels (clothes only)
  02 5112813
Brussels (home furnishings
  only) 02 5120447
Gent 092 240819

FRANCE
Paris
94 rue de Rennes 1 45 48 43 89
95 rue de Raymond Poincaré
  1 45 01 24 73
261 rue Saint Honoré
  1 42 86 84 13
Galeries Lafayette, 40 bld

Haussmann
second floor (clothes only)
1 42 82 34 56
fifth floor (home furnishings
  only) 1 42 82 04 11
Au Printemps, 64 bld
  Haussmann
second floor (clothes only)
1 42 82 52 10
seventh floor (home
furnishings only)
1 42 82 44 20
Au Printemps, Center
  Commercial Vélizy
  Avenue de l'Europe, Vélizy,
  Villacoublay
  Niveau 2 (clothes and home
  furnishings) 1 30 70 87 66
Au Printemps, Center
  Commercial Parly 2
  Avenue Charles de Gaulle, Le
  Chesnay
  Niveau 1 (home furnishings
  only) 1 39 54 22 44
  Niveau 2 (clothes only)
  1 39 54 22 44
Aix-en-Provence 42 27 31 92
Bordeaux 56 44 10 30
Clemont-Ferrand 73 31 22 05
Dijon 80 30 04 44
Lille 20 06 90 06
Lyon 78 37 18 19
Montpelier 67 60 75 75
Nancy 83 35 21 09
Nantes 40 73 17 18
Nice 93 16 06 93
Rouen 35 70 20 02
Strasbourg 88 75 18 90
Toulon 94 21 89 58
Toulouse 61 21 38 85

GERMANY
Augsburg 0821 154021
Berlin (home furnishings only)
 030 8826201
Berlin (clothes only)
 030 8824934
Berlin (Kadewe) 030 2183016
Bielefeld 0521 177188
Bonn 0228 654908
Bremen 0421 170443
Cologne 0221 2580470
Dortmund 0231 141009
Düsseldorf 0211 8648732
Essen 0201 200482
Frankfurt 069 288791
Hamburg 040 371173
Hanover 0511 326919
Heidelberg 06 22 1189851
Karlsruhe 0721 25968
Munich 089 2608224
Münster 0251 42272
Nuremberg 0911 24518
Stuttgart 0711 2261064
Wiesbaden 0611 302086

ITALY
Milan 2 86463532

LUXEMBOURG
Luxembourg 221 320

NETHERLANDS
Amsterdam 020 6228087
Arnhem
 085 430250 (026 4430250)
Eindhoven 040 (2)435022
Groningen 050 (3)185060
The Hague 070 3600540
Maastricht 043 (3)250972
Rotterdam 010 4148535
Utrecht 030 (2)313051

SPAIN
Barcelona 341 25490

SWITZERLAND
Basel 061 2619757
Bern 031 3120696
Geneva (clothes only)
 22 33113494
Geneva (home furnishings only)
 22 33103048
Zurich 01 2211394

ASIA
HONG KONG SHOPS IN
SHOPS
Seibu 852 2801 7849
Sogo 852 2891 1787

JAPAN
Ginza 03 3571 5011
Yagoto 052 836 7086
Kichijoji 0422 21 1203
Jiyugaoka 03 3724 0051
Yokohama LMP 045 222 5308
Shibuya 03 3464 5011
Futako Tamagawa
 03 3708 3151
Gifu Melsa 0582 66 3136
Fukuoka Tenjin 092 716 7415

JAPAN SHOPS IN SHOPS
TOKYO
Mitsukoshi Nihonbashi
 03 3241 5617
Mitsukoshi Ikebukuro
 03 3987 6074
Tokyu 03 3477 3836
Keio Shinjuku 03 3344 0080
Mitsukoshi Ginza 03 3561 4050
Tobu Ikebukuro 03 3980 0041

REST OF JAPAN
Mitsukoshi Yokohama
 045 323 1683

Saikaya Kawasaki
 0044 211 8581
Saikaya Yokosuka
 0468 23 1234
Chiba Mitsukoshi 043 227
4731
Mitsukoshi Bandai
 025 243 6333
Sapporo Tokyu 011 212 2658
Kintetsu Abeno 06 625 2332
Hankyu Umeda 06 365 0793
Kawanishi Hankyu
 0727 56 1622
Mitsukoshi Hiroshima
 082 241 5055
Hiroshima Sogo 082 225 2955
Hakata Izutsuya 092 452 2181
Fukuoka Tamaya 092 271 6588
Nagoya Mitsukoshi
 052 252 1838
Matsuzakaya Nagoyacki
 052 565 4339
Seishin Sogo 078 992 1586
Kobe Ilankyu 078 360 7528
Daimaru Kobe 078 333 4079
Tama Sogo 0423 39 2450
Kintetsu Kyoto
 075 365 8024/8013
Be Me Machida Daimaru
 0427 24 8174
Sanyo Himeji 0792 23 4792
Tenmaya Fukuyama
 0849 27 2214
Mitsukoshi Matsuyama
 0899 46 4829
Saikaya Fujisawa 0466 27 1111
Matsuzukaya Yokkaichi
 0593 551241
Cita Tokiwa 0975 33 1741
Bon Belta Narita 0476 23 3236
Hanamatsu Matsubishi
 053 452 2941
Kagoshima Mitsukoshi
 0992 39 4635

Saga Tamaya 0952 28 0608
Kintetsu Nara 0742 30 2751
Kokura Izutsuya 093 522 2627

SINGAPORE
SHOPS IN SHOPS
Sogo 65 334 1014
Isetan Scotts 65 735 0495

TAIWAN
SHOPS IN SHOPS
Ta-Lee Isetan 886 7 241 8860
Pacific Sogo 886 2 740 9662
Shin Kong Mitsukoshi
 886 2 382 4859

Sources and Suppliers

UNITED STATES

FABRICS AND TEXTILES

ABC Carpet & Home
888 Broadway
New York
NY 10003
212 473 3000

André Bon
979 Third Avenue
New York
NY 10022
212 355 4012

Clarence House
979 Third Avenue
New York
NY 10022
212 753 2890

Liberty of London
108 West 39th Street
New York
NY 10018
212 391 2150

Pierre Deux Fabrics
870 Madison Avenue
New York
NY 10021
212 570 9343

Scalamandre
950 Third Avenue
New York
NY 10022
212 980 3888

J Schumacher & Company
79 Madison Avenue
New York
NY 10016
212 213 7900

Standard Trimming Co.
306 East 62nd Street
New York
NY 10021
212 355 4012

PAINTS AND PAPERS

Decorating Centers
1555 Third Avenue
New York
NY 10028
212 289 6300

2475 Broadway
New York
NY 10025
212 769 1440

Sam Flax
12 West 20th Street
New York
NY 10011
212 620 3038

425 Park Avenue
New York
NY 10022
212 620 3060

Liberty Paint Co.
969 Columbia Street
Hudson
NY 12534
518 828 4060

Pearl Paint Co.
308 Canal Street
New York
NY 10013
212 431 7932

Wolf Paint and Paper
Janovic Plaza
771 Ninth Avenue
New York
NY 10019
212 245 3241

Janovic Plaza
1150 Third Avenue
New York
NY 10022
212 772 1400

UNITED KINGDOM

FABRICS AND TEXTILES

The Blue Door
77 Church Road
London SW13 9HH
0181 748 9785

Colefax and Fowler
118 Garratt Lane
London SW18 4DJ
0181 874 6484
Chintz fabrics

The Conran Shop
Michelin House
81 Fulham Road
London SW3 6RB
0171 589 7401
For fabrics

George Weil
Showroom
18 Hanson Street
London W1P 7DB
0171 580 3763

Mail order
Reading Arch Road
Redhill
Surrey RH1 1H6
For dyes, fabric paints and fabrics

Hess and Co
7 Warple Mews
Warple Way
London W3 0RS
0181 746 1366
For interlinings and linings

John Lewis Partnership plc
Oxford Street
London W1Z 1EX
0171 629 7711
Excellent haberdashery and lighting departments; branches nationwide

Ian Mankin
109 Regent's Park Road
London NW1 8UR
0171 722 0997
For fabrics

Just Fabrics
Burford Antique Center
Cheltenham Road
Burford
Oxfordshire OX8 4JA
01993 823391
Plain-colored chintzes and other fabrics

Liberty
210–220 Regent Street
London W1R 6AH
0171 734 1234
Plain and patterned cotton fabrics, silks and linens

The Natural Fabric Company
Wessex Place
127 High Street
Hungerford
Berkshire RG17 0DL
01468 684002

VV Rouleaux
10 Symons Street
Sloane Square
London SW3 2TJ
0171 730 3125
For an exceptional selection of ribbons, braids, cords, tassels and other trimmings

Sanderson
112–120 Brompton Road
London SW3 1JJ
0171 584 3344
Fabrics, William Morris prints, furniture

PAINTS AND PAPERS
J. W. Bollom
13 Theobald's Road
London WC1X 8FN
0171 242 0313
General painting supplies

314 Old Brompton Road
London SW5 9JH
(Showroom)

C. Brewer
327 Putney Bridge Road
London SW15 2PG
0181 788 9335
General painting supplies. Various branches in S. E. England

Brodie and Middleton Ltd
68 Drury Lane
London WC2B 5SP
0171 836 3289
Pigments and paints

Cornelissen and Son Ltd
105 Great Russell Street
London WC1B 3RY
0171 636 1045
Pigments and brushes

Craig & Rose plc
172 Leith Walk
Edinburgh EH6 5ER
0131 554 1131
Glazes, specialist brushes. Stockists nationwide.

Daler-Rowney Ltd
PO Box 10
Southern Industrial Estate
Bracknell
Berkshire RG12 8ST
01344 424621
Artists' materials

The English Stamp Company
Sunnydown
Worth Matravers
Dorset BH19 3JP
01929 439117
Farrow & Ball
Uddens Trading Estate
Wimbourne
Dorset BH21 7NL
01202 876141
National Trust range of historical paints

Foxell & James Ltd
57 Farringdon Road
London EC1M 3JH
0171 405 0152
Varnishes, primers, paints, glazes, floor finishes, rabbit-skin glue, whiting, metal powders

Green & Stone
259 Kings Road
London SW3 5EL
0171 352 0837
Artists' materials

W. Habberley Meadows Ltd
5 Saxon Way
Chelmsley Wood
Birmingham B37 5AY
0121 770 2905
Artists' paints and brushes, gilding materials

J. T. Keep & Co.
13 Theobalds Road
London WC1X 8SN
0171 242 7578
General decorating suppliers

Lyn Le Grice Stencil Design Ltd
The Stencil House
53 Chapel Street
Penzanze
Cornwall TR18 4AS
01736 64193
Stencil books, kits and materials

John Myland
80 Norwood High Street
London SE27 9NW
0181 670 9161
Artists' brushes and materials
Paint Magic
116 Sheen Road
Richmond
Surrey TW9 1UR
0181 940 5503
Paint effect kits, colorwash, woodwash, crackle-glaze, stenciling supplies

The Paint Service Co. Ltd
19 Eccleston Street
London SW1W 9LX
0171 730 6408

Papers and Paints
4 Park Walk
London SW10 0AD
0171 352 8626

Pavilion Stencils
6a Howe Street
Edinburgh EH3 6TD
0131 225 3590
Stenciling supplies

E. Ploton Ltd
273 Archway Road
London N6 5AA
0181 348 0315
Metallic powders, gilding materials

Potmolen Paint
27 Woodstock Industrial Estate
Warminster
Wiltshire BA12 9DX
01985 213960
Paints and finishes suitable for old buildings

J. H. Ratcliffe & Co. (Paints) Ltd
135a Linaker Street
Southport PR8 5DF
01704 537999
Transparent oil glaze

The Shaker Shop
25 Harcourt Street
London W1H 1DT
0171 724 7672
Old Village buttermilk paints
Stuart R. Stevenson
68 Clerkenwell Road
London EC1M 5QA
0171 253 1693
Gilding materials

Acknowledgments

The publishers would like to thank the following people for their invaluable help in the production of this book: Mary Batten for her advice and support; Jemima Dyson for her styling and editorial assistance; Chris Churchley for her help; Petra Boase for designing the appliqué tablecloth (pages 156–7) and the braided rag rug (pages 196–7); Clement Barbic for decorating the red dining room (pages 182–91) and the terracotta bathroom (192–9); Derek Sutton for his help in decorating the other rooms.

Joss Graham Oriental Textiles
10 Eccleston Street
London SW1W 9LT
0171 730 4370

HRW Antiques
4a Kings Avenue
London SW4
0171 978 1026

Graham and Green
4, 7 & 10 Elgin Crescent
London W11 2JA
0171 727 4594

Perez Antique Carpets Gallery
150 Wandworth Bridge Road
London SW6 2LH
0171 589 2199

David Wainwright
251 Portobello Road
London W11
0171 792 1988

The Dining Room Shop
62–4 White Hart Lane
London SW13
0181 878 1020

Ian Mankin
109 Regents Park Road
London NW1 8UR
0171 722 0997

Homeline
33 Parkway
London NW1
0171 485 0744

Harwood Antiques
24 Lower Richmond Road
London SW15 1JP
0181 788 7444

Gallery of Antique Costumes and Textiles
2 Church Street
London NW8
0171 723 9981

Thomas Goode
19 South Audley Street
London W1Y 6BN
0171 499 2823

The Barnes Gallery
51 Church Road
London SW13 9HH
0181 741 1277

Tulissio de Beaumont
Decorative Antiques
277 Lillie Road
London SW6 7PN
0171 385 0156

Farrow and Ball Paint Suppliers
Uddens Trading Estate
Wimborne
Dorset
BH21 7NL
01202 876141

The publishers would like to thank the following companies for permission to reproduce photographs in this book:
8–9 The Laura Ashley Archive; 10 top left Richard Bryant/Arcaid; 10 top right Jacqui Hurst; 10 left of centre The Laura Ashley Archive; 10 bottom left Simon Upton/Robert Harding Picture Library; 10 bottom right Anne Hyde; 11 top left Anne Hyde; 11 top right Anne Hyde; 11 left of centre Rupert Horrox; 11 bottom left Andrew Payne/Belle/Arcaid; 11 bottom right Anne Hyde; 13 The Laura Ashley Archive; 15 Anne Hyde; 17 Richard Waite/Arcaid. designer Louise Cotier; 18 Simon Brown/Robert Harding Picture Library; 19 Andreas von Einsiedel/Robert Harding Picture Library; 23 The Laura Ashley Archive; 24 Geoff Lung/Belle/Arcaid; 25 Robert Harding Picture Library; 39 Richard Bryant/Arcaid, by kind permission of The Mount Vernon Ladies' Association of the Union; 40 National Trust Photographic Library/Bill Batten; 41 The Laura Ashley Archive; 42 Richard Bryant/Arcaid; 50 top left Jacqui Hurst; 50 top right Rupert Horrox; 50 left of centre Jacqui Hurst; 50 right of centre Jacqui Hurst; 50 bottom left Rupert Horrox; 50 bottom right Anne Hyde; 51 top right Lucinda Lambton/Arcaid; 51 left of centre Anne Hyde; 51 bottom left Rupert Horrox; 52 National Trust Photographic Library/Rupert Truman; 55 Richard Bryant/Arcaid; 56 The Laura Ashley Archive; 59 Jan Baldwin/Robert Harding Picture Library; 61 The Laura Ashley Archive; 80 top right Anne Hyde; 80 left of centre Lucinda Lambton/Arcaid; 80 right of centre National Trust Photographic Library/Andreas von Einsiedel; 80 bottom left Jacqui Hurst; 80 bottom right Jacqui Hurst; 81 top right Richard Bryant/Arcaid; 81 left of centre Anne Hyde; 81 bottom left Polly Wreford/Robert Harding Picture Library; 81 bottom right Anne Hyde; 83 Richard Bryant/Arcaid; 85 Fritz von der Schulenburg/Robert Harding Picture Library; 86 Andreas von Einsiedel/Robert Harding Picture Library; 87 Andreas von Einsiedel/Robert Harding Picture Library; 88 The Laura Ashley Archive; 108 top left Anne Hyde; 108 top right Jacqui Hurst; 108 left of centre The Laura Ashley Archive; 108 right of centre The Laura Ashley Archive; 108 bottom left National Trust Photographic Library/Nick Meers; 108 bottom right David Fowler/Arcaid; 109 top right National Trust Photographic Library/Andreas von Einsiedel; 109 left of centre Simon Page-Ritchie/Robert Harding Picture Library; 109 bottom left Mark Fiennes/Arcaid; 109 bottom right Anne Hyde; 113 The Laura Ashley Archive; 114 Richard Bryant/Arcaid; 116 National Trust Photographic Library/Andreas von Einsiedel; 138 top left Anne Hyde; 138 top right Robert O'Dea/Arcaid; 138 bottom left Jacqui Hurst; 138 bottom right Anne Hyde; 138 left of centre Lucinda Lambton/Arcaid; 138 right of centre Robert Harding Picture Library; 139 top left Anne Hyde; 139 left of centre Christopher Drake/Robert Harding Picture Library; 139 bottom left Anne Hyde; 139 bottom left Jacqui Hurst; 143 Jacqui Hurst; 145 The Laura Ashley Archive; 147 The Laura Ashley Archive; 149 Annet Held/Arcaid; 151 Farrell Grehan/Arcaid; 172 top left Trevor Wood/Robert Harding Picture Library; 172 right of centre Christopher Drake/Robert Harding Picture Library; 172 bottom left Tom Leighton/Robert Harding Picture Library; 172 bottom right Walter Rawlings/Robert Harding Picture Library; 173 top left 173 top right Debbie Patterson/Robert Harding Picture Library; 173 left of centre Jan Baldwin/Robert Harding Picture Library; 173 bottom left Jacqui Hurst; 173 bottom right Chrisopher Drake/Robert Harding Picture Library; 175 Richard Bryant/Arcaid; 177 Richard Waite/Arcaid, designer Louise Cotier; 179 David Churchill/Arcaid; 181 The Laura Ashley Archive.

Index